Flamingo Adult Coloring Book

This Coloring book belongs to:

_____

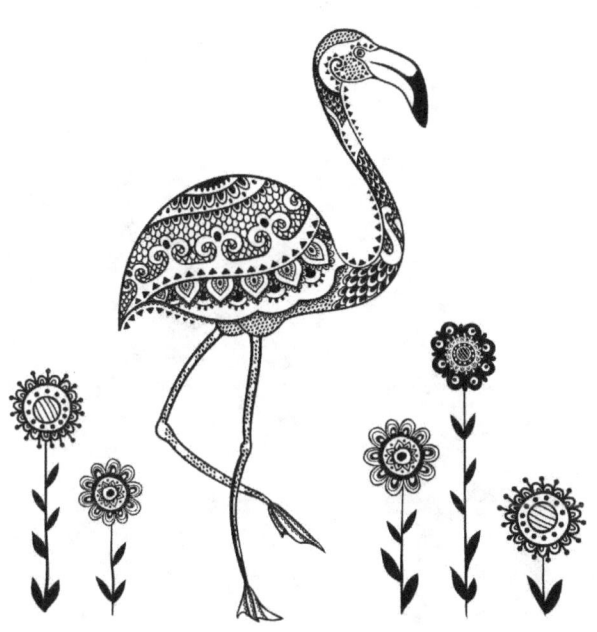

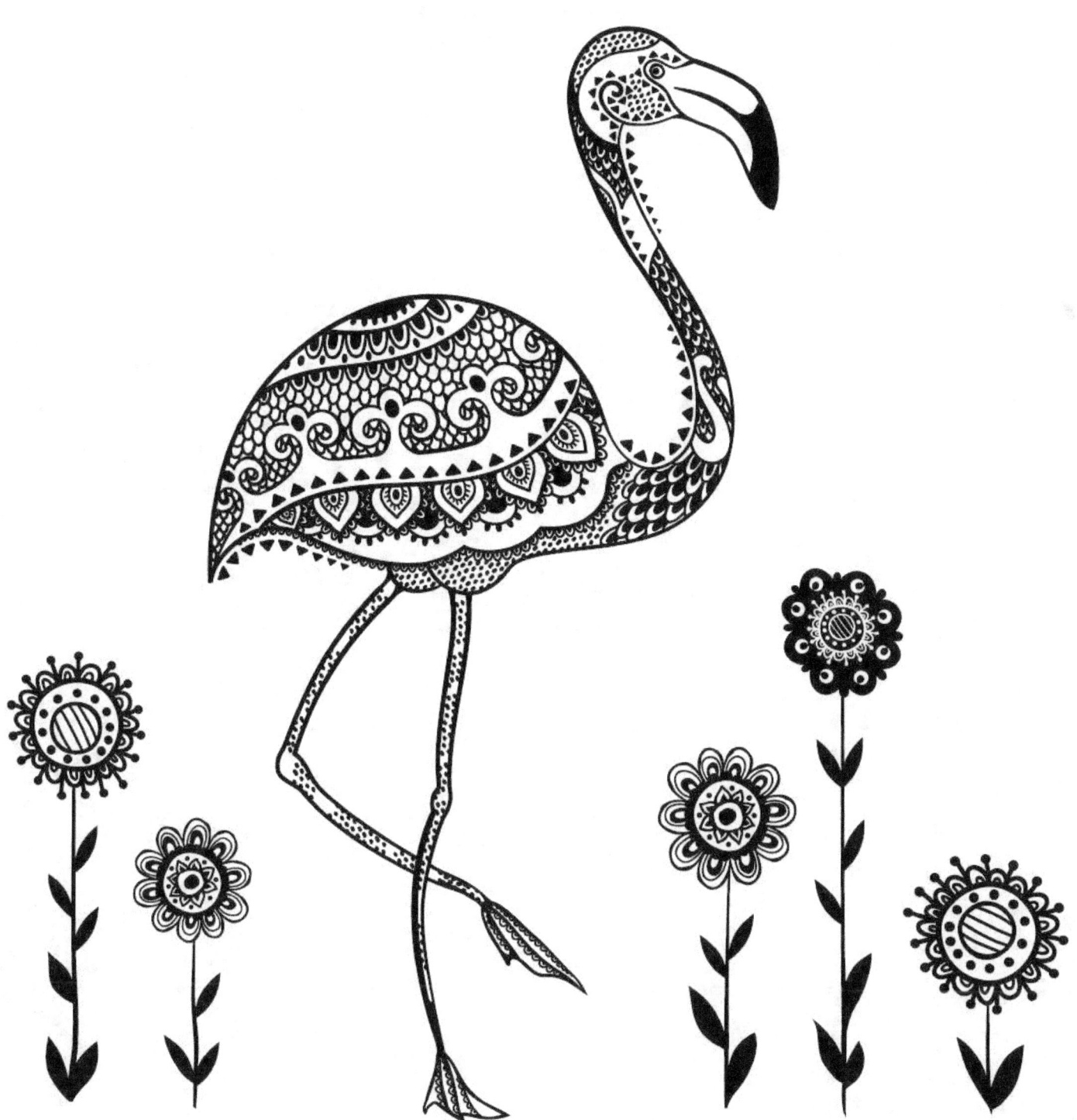

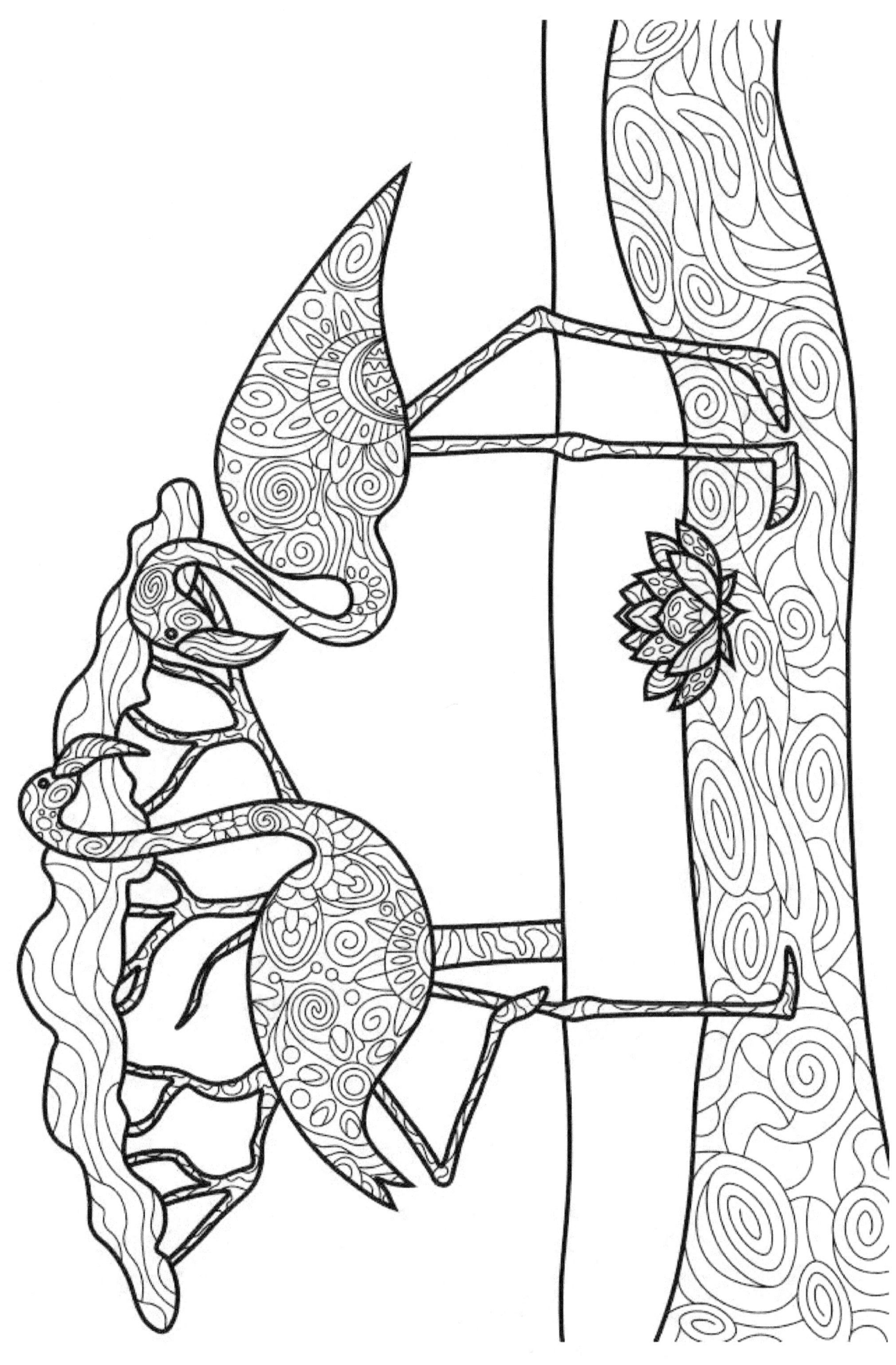

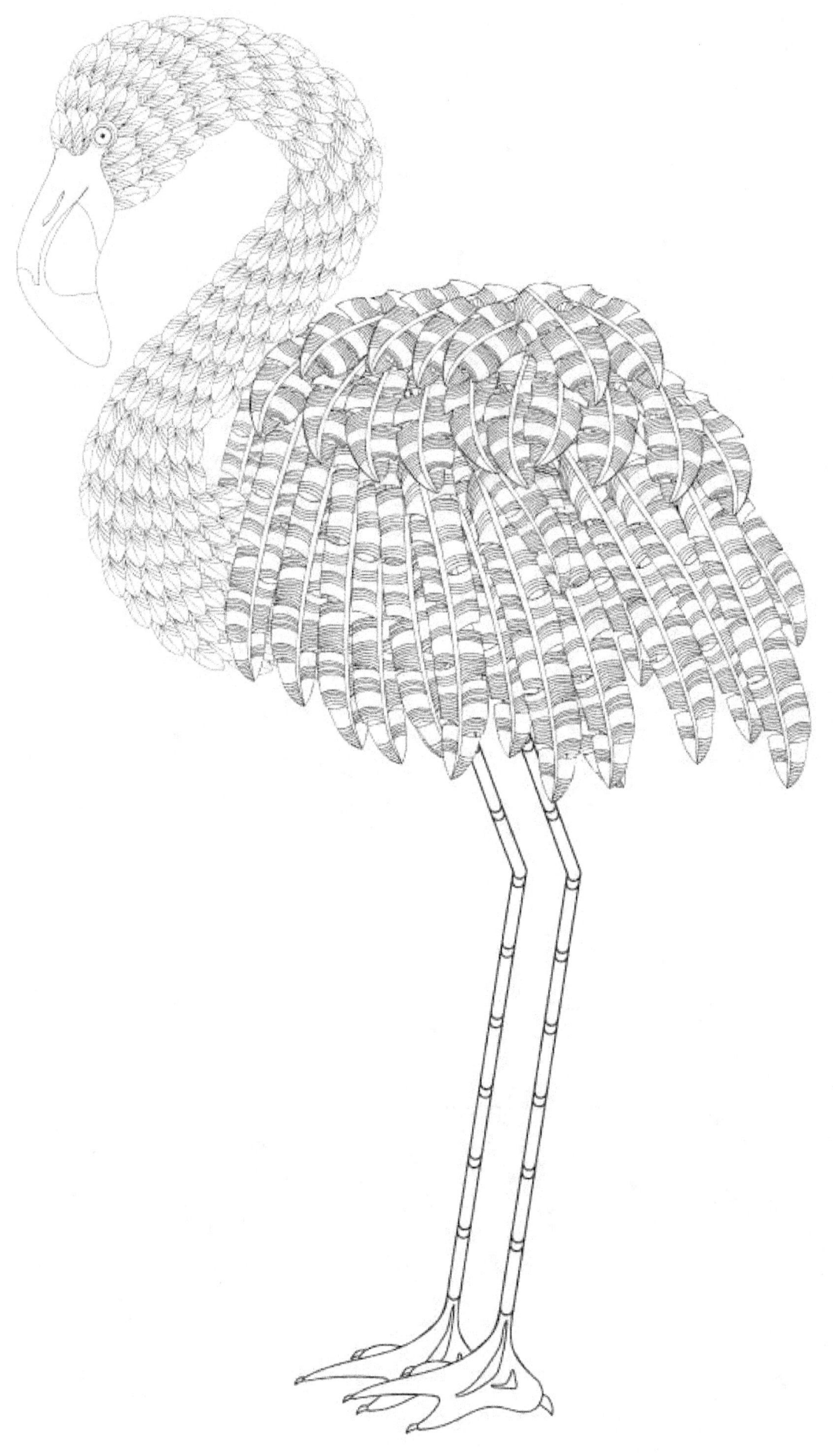

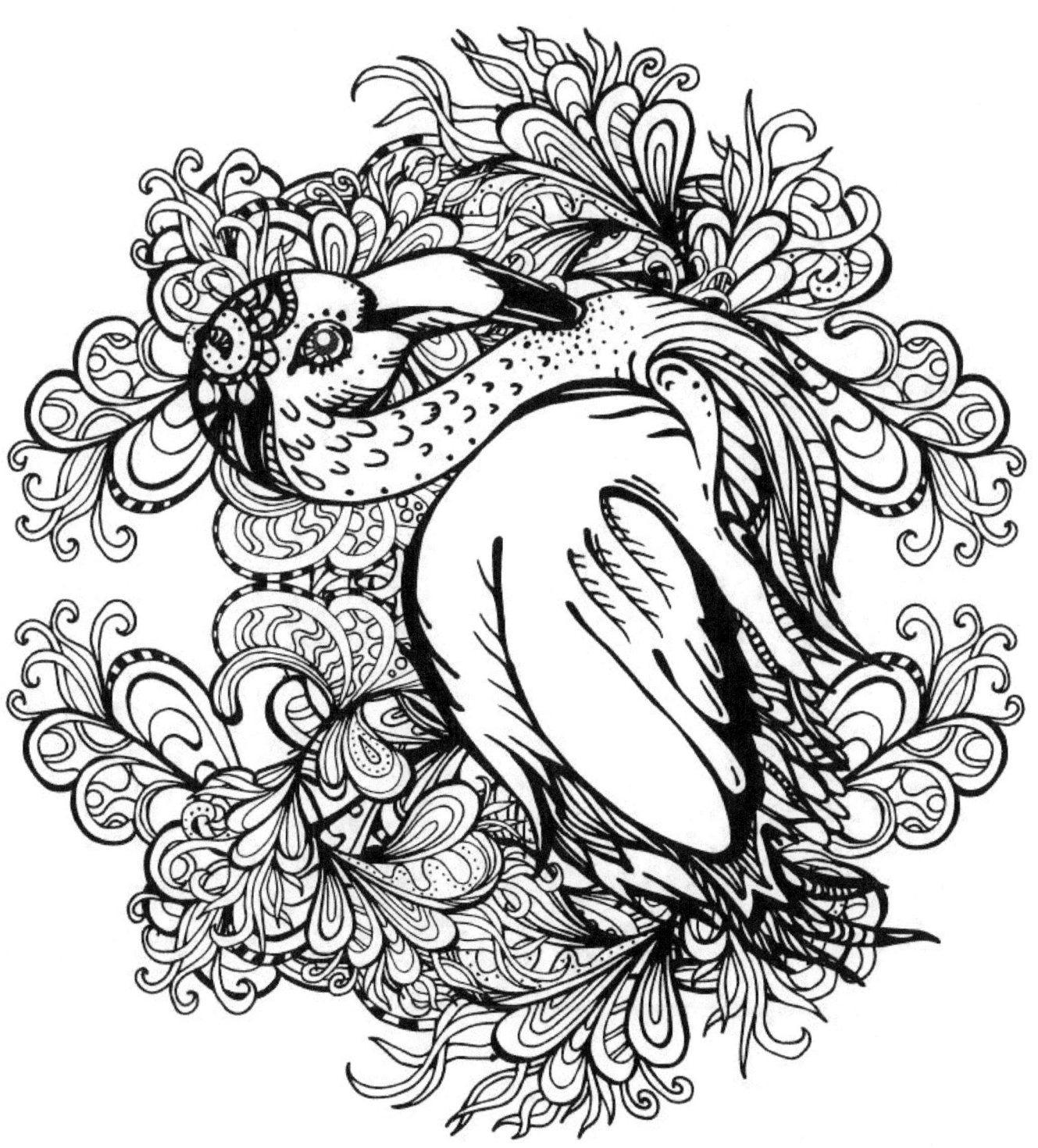

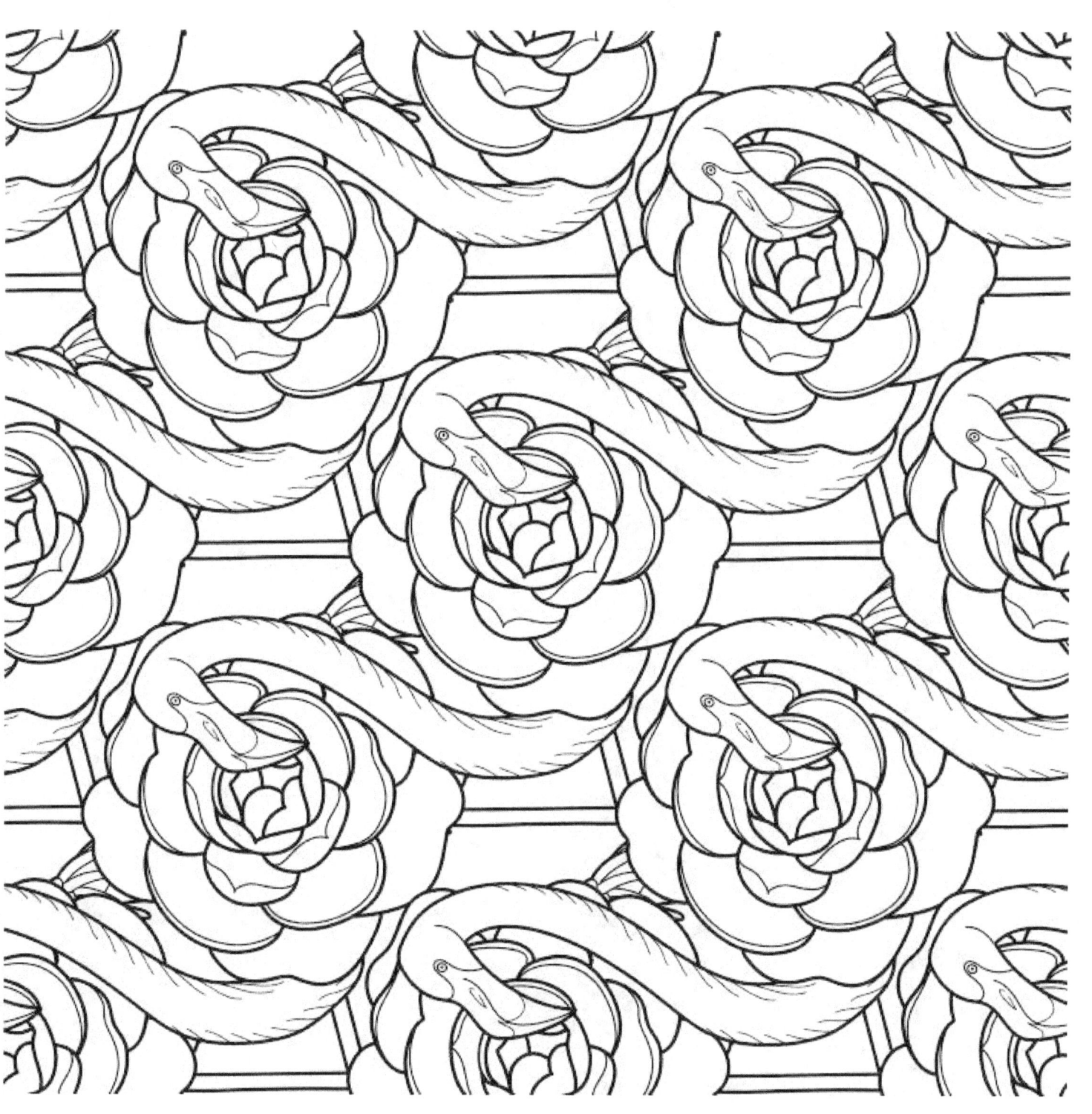

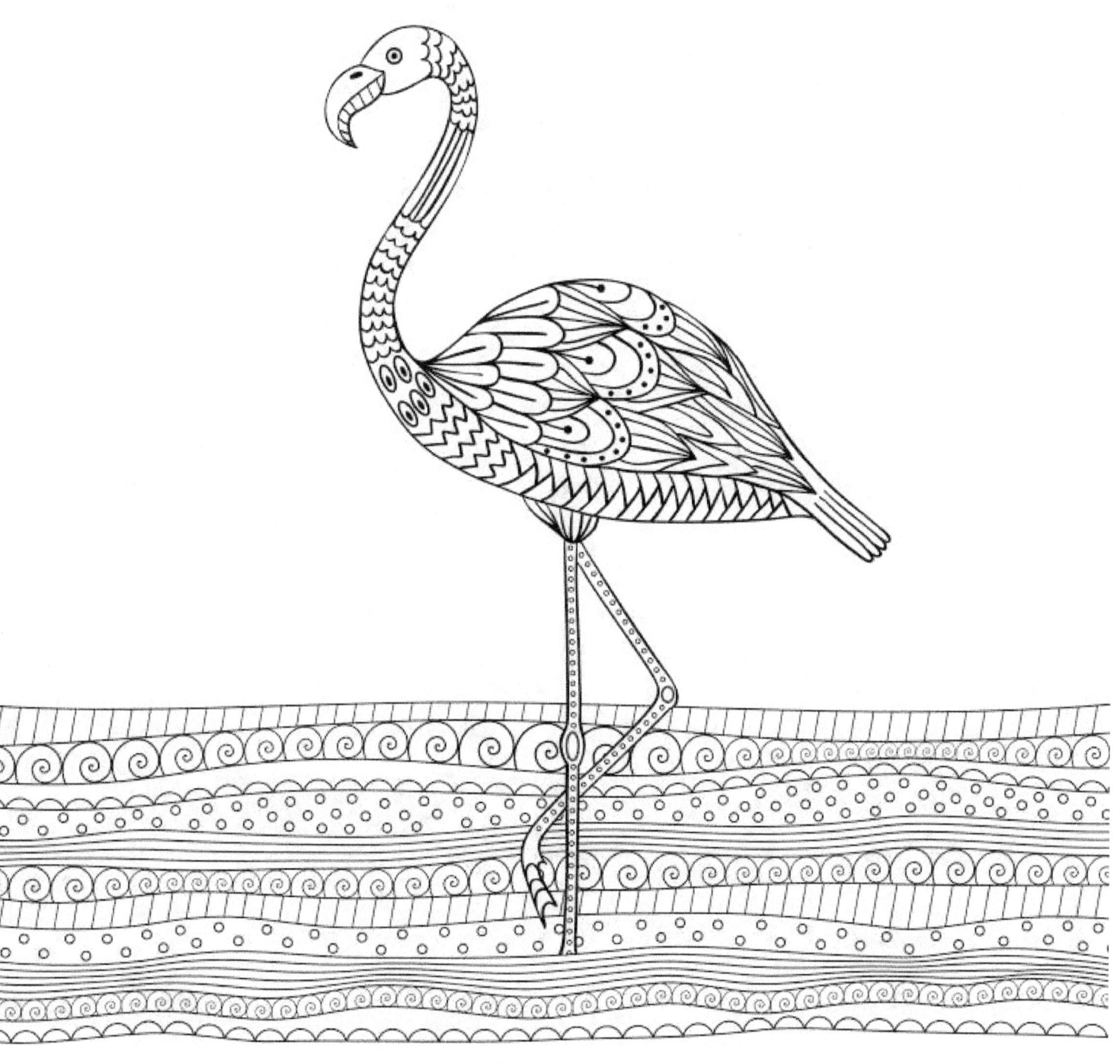

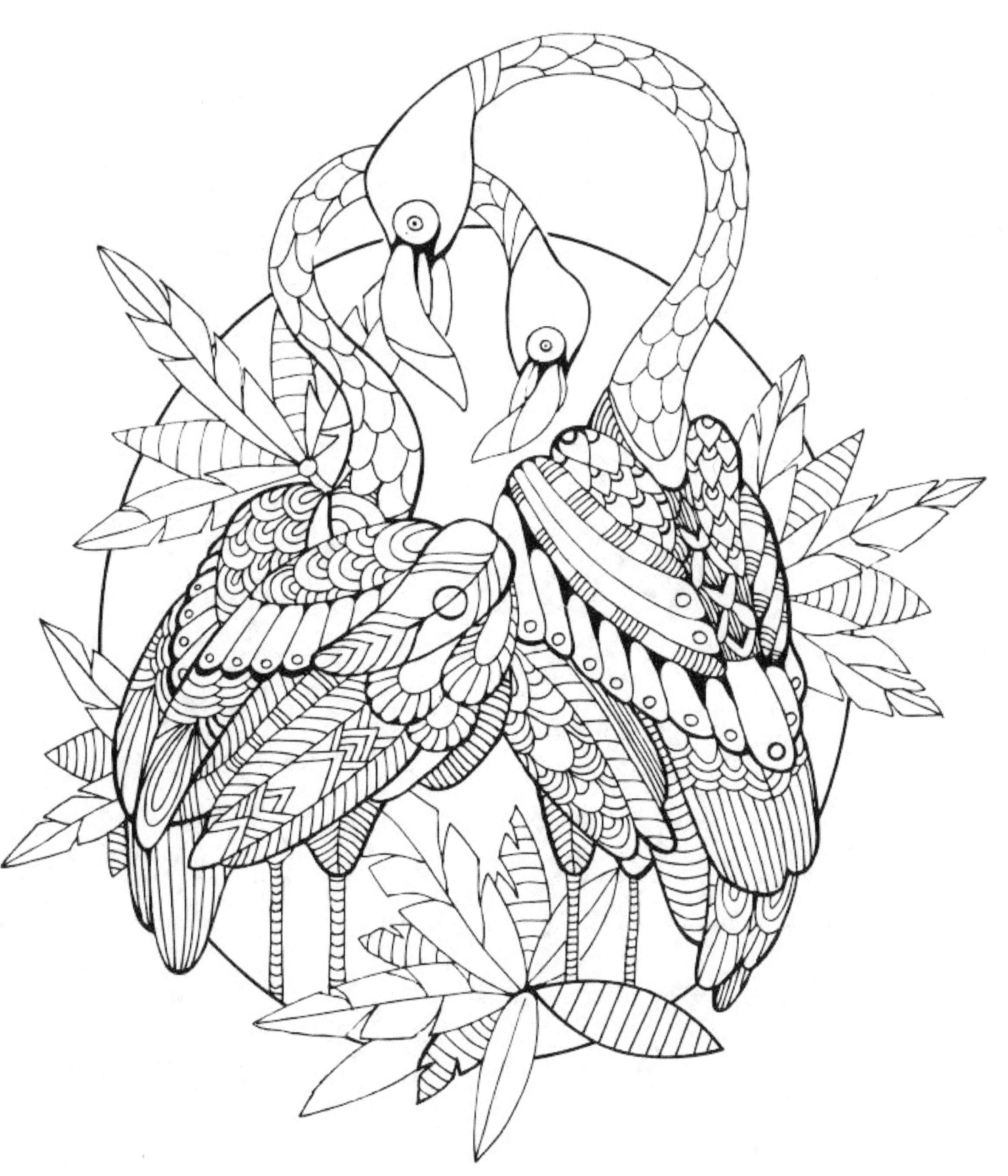

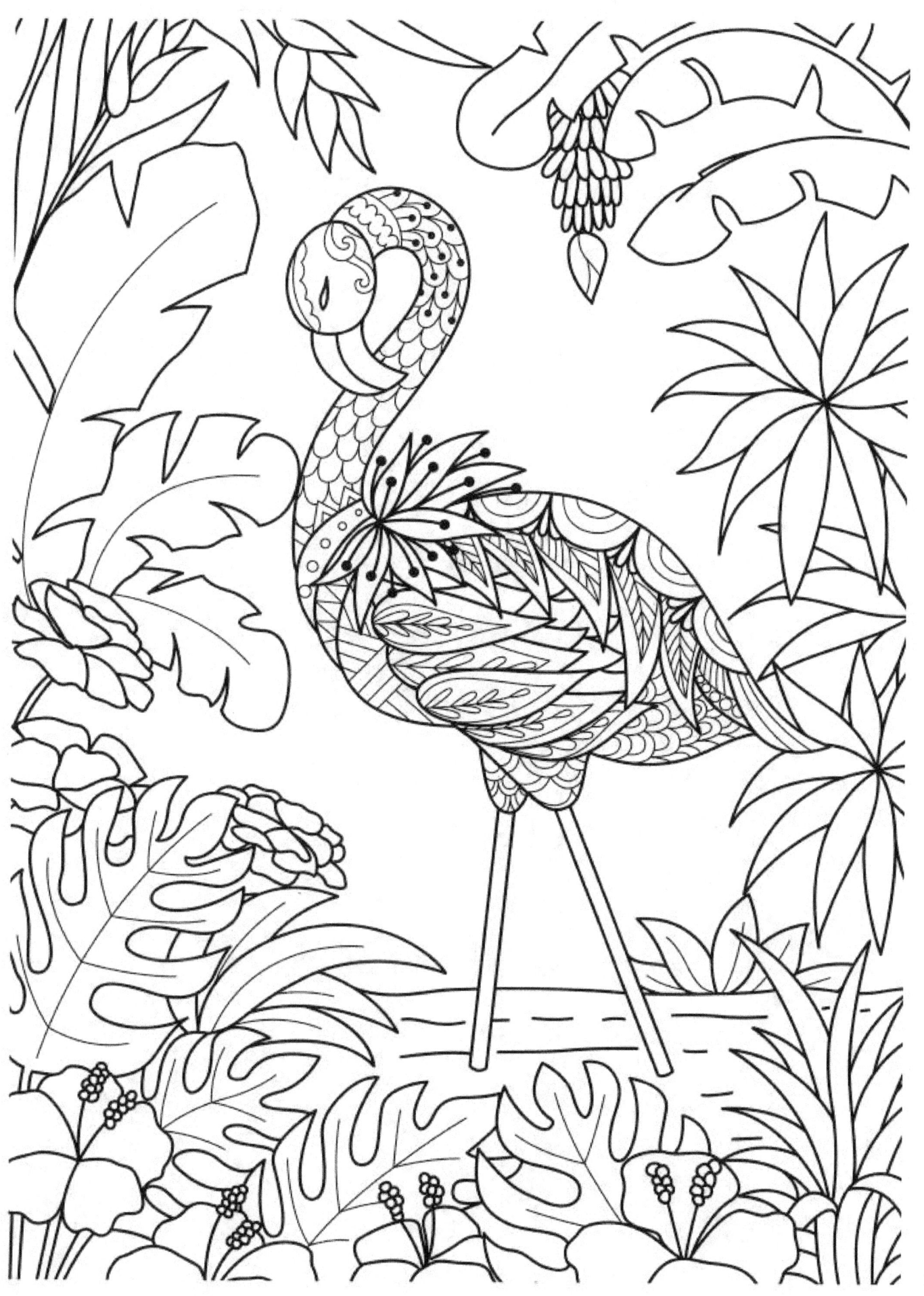

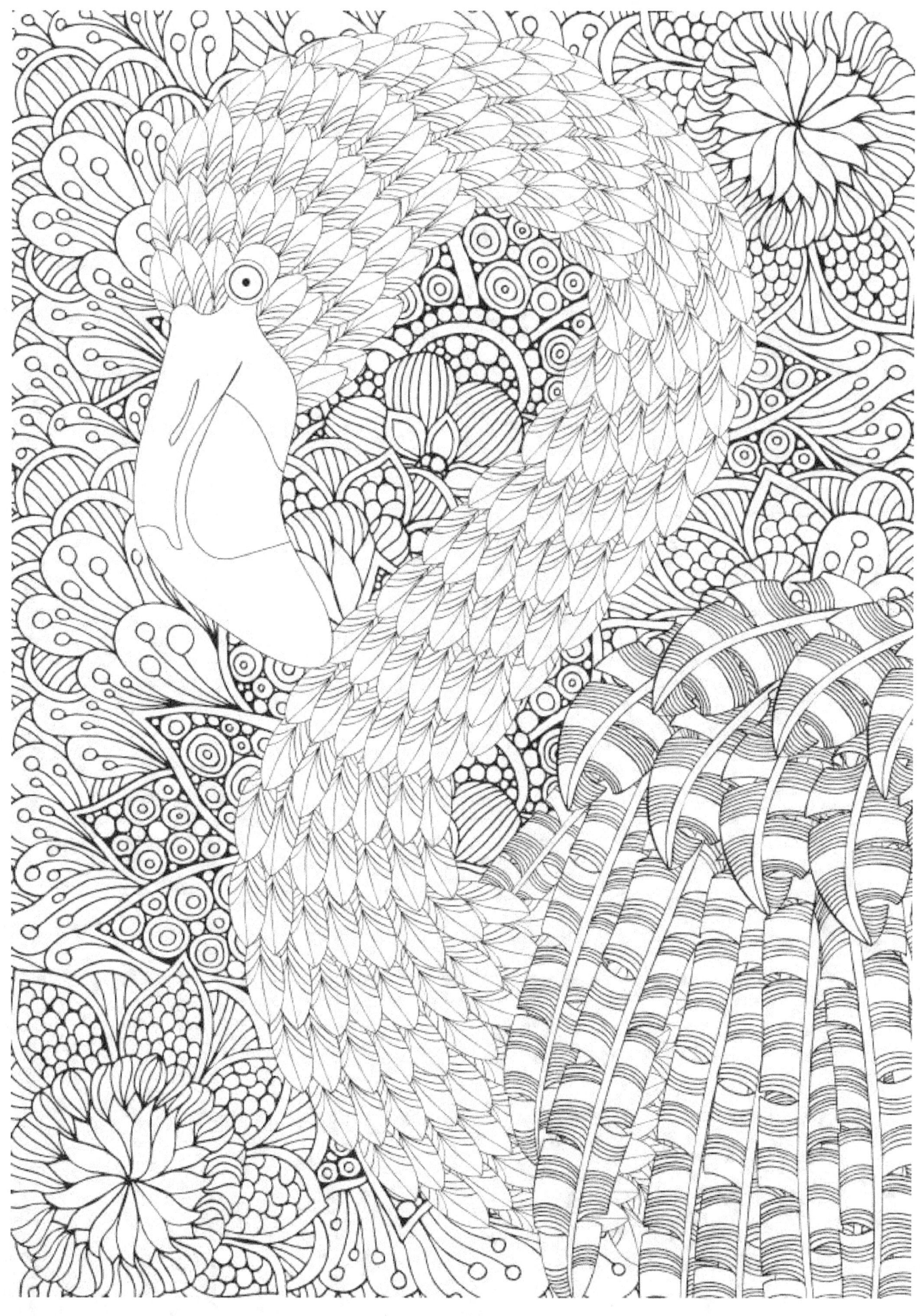

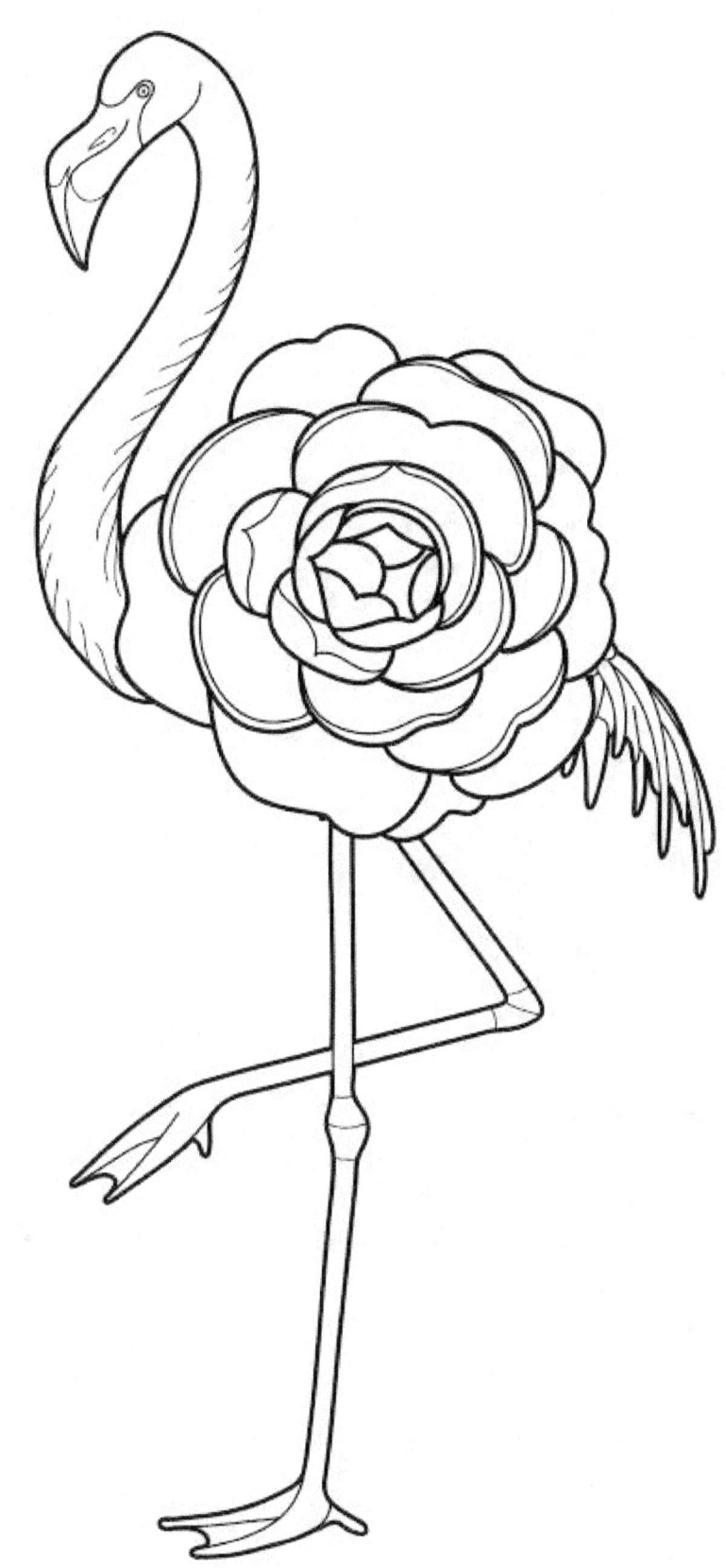

Example of different color shades to use for your flamingo coloring pages.

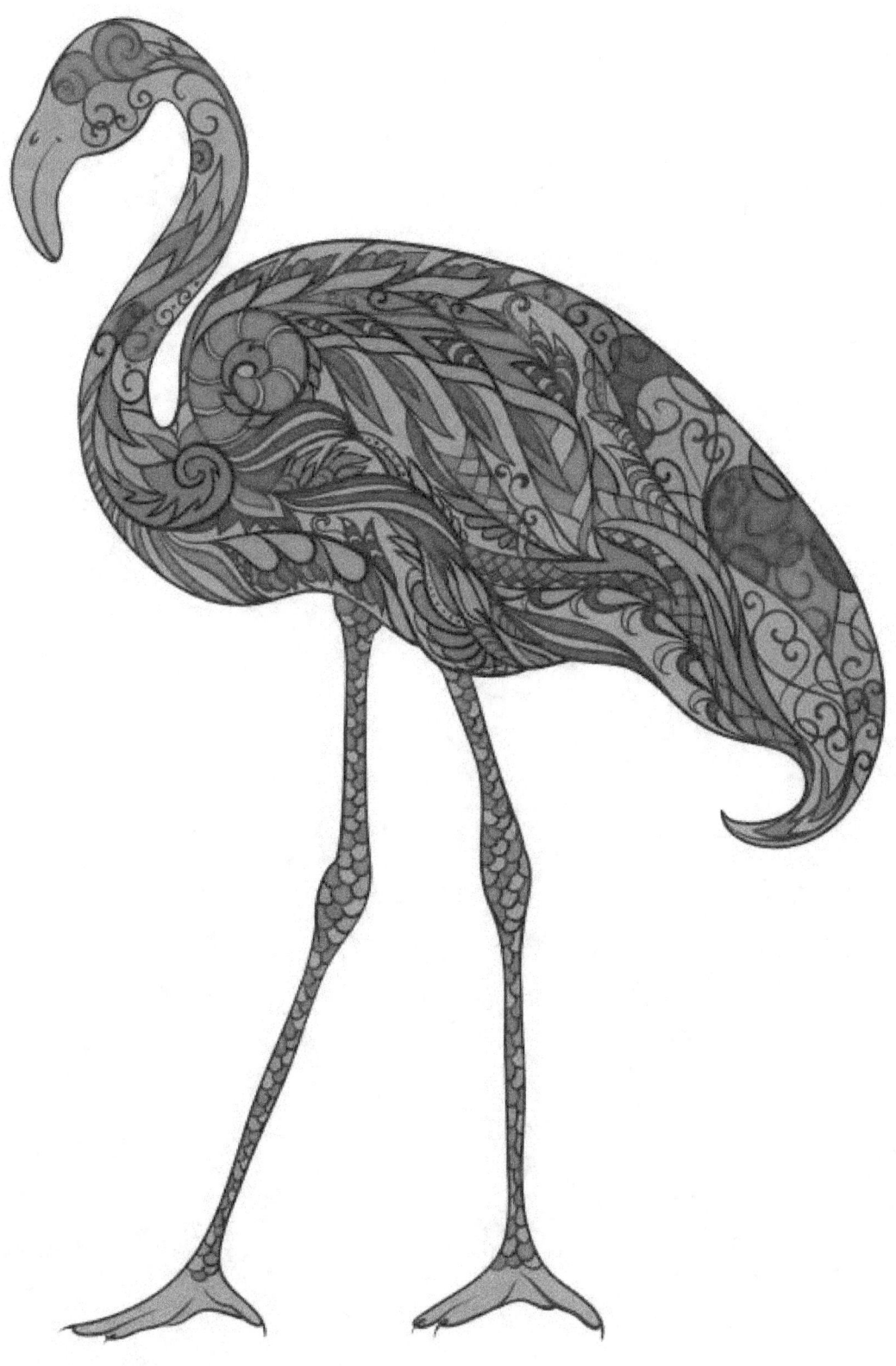

SURPRISE BONUS! FROGS AND SEA TURTLES.

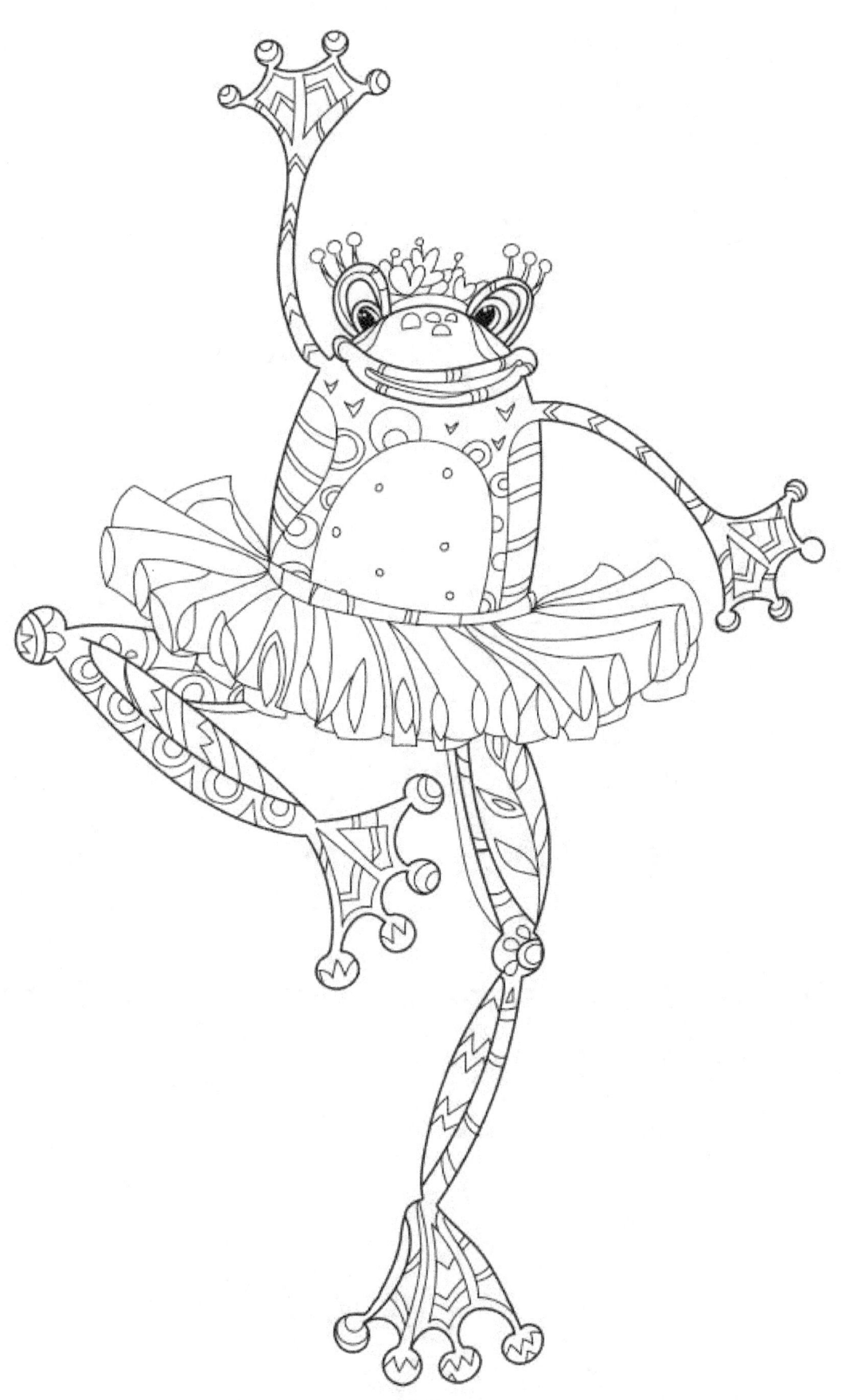

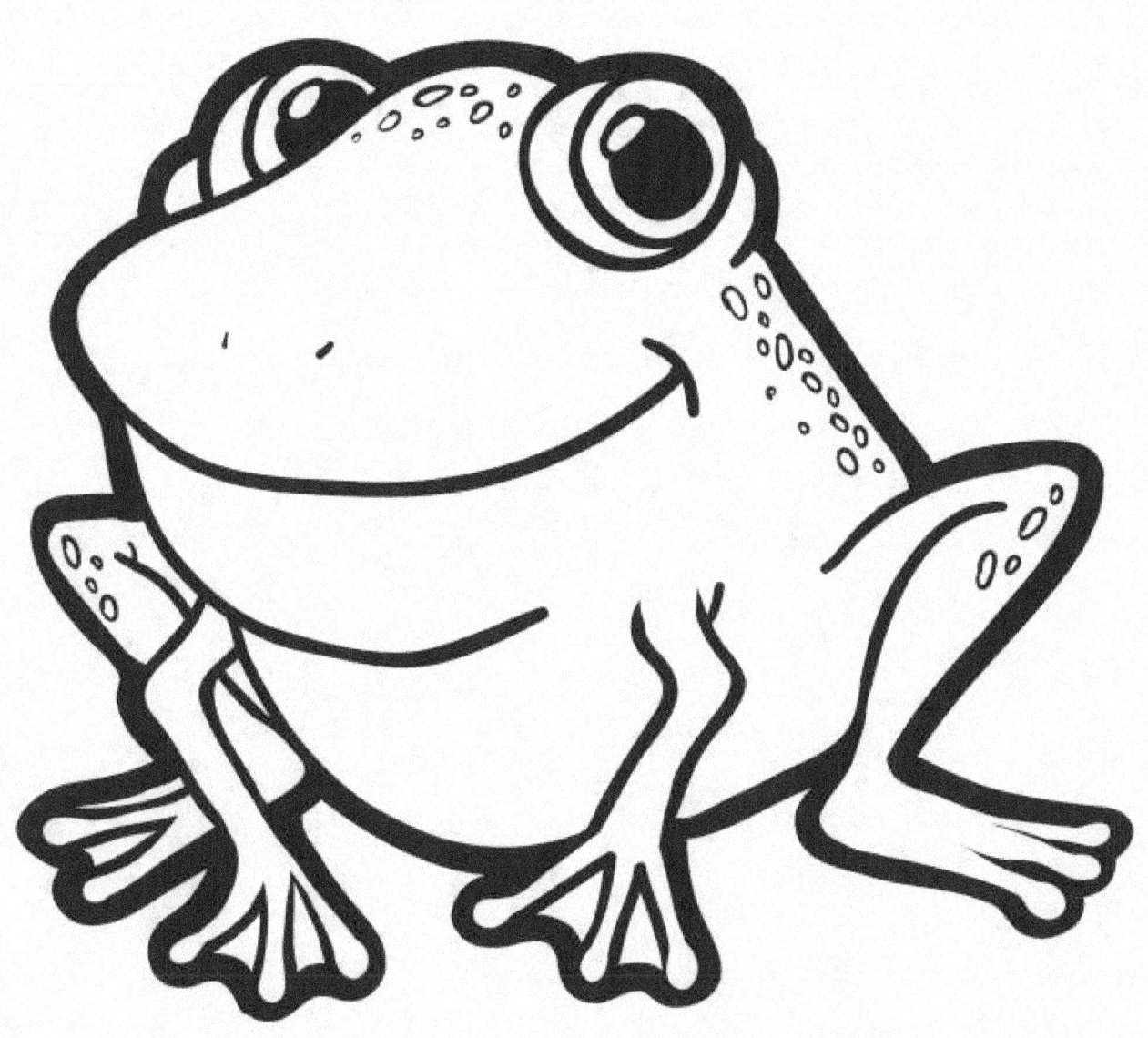

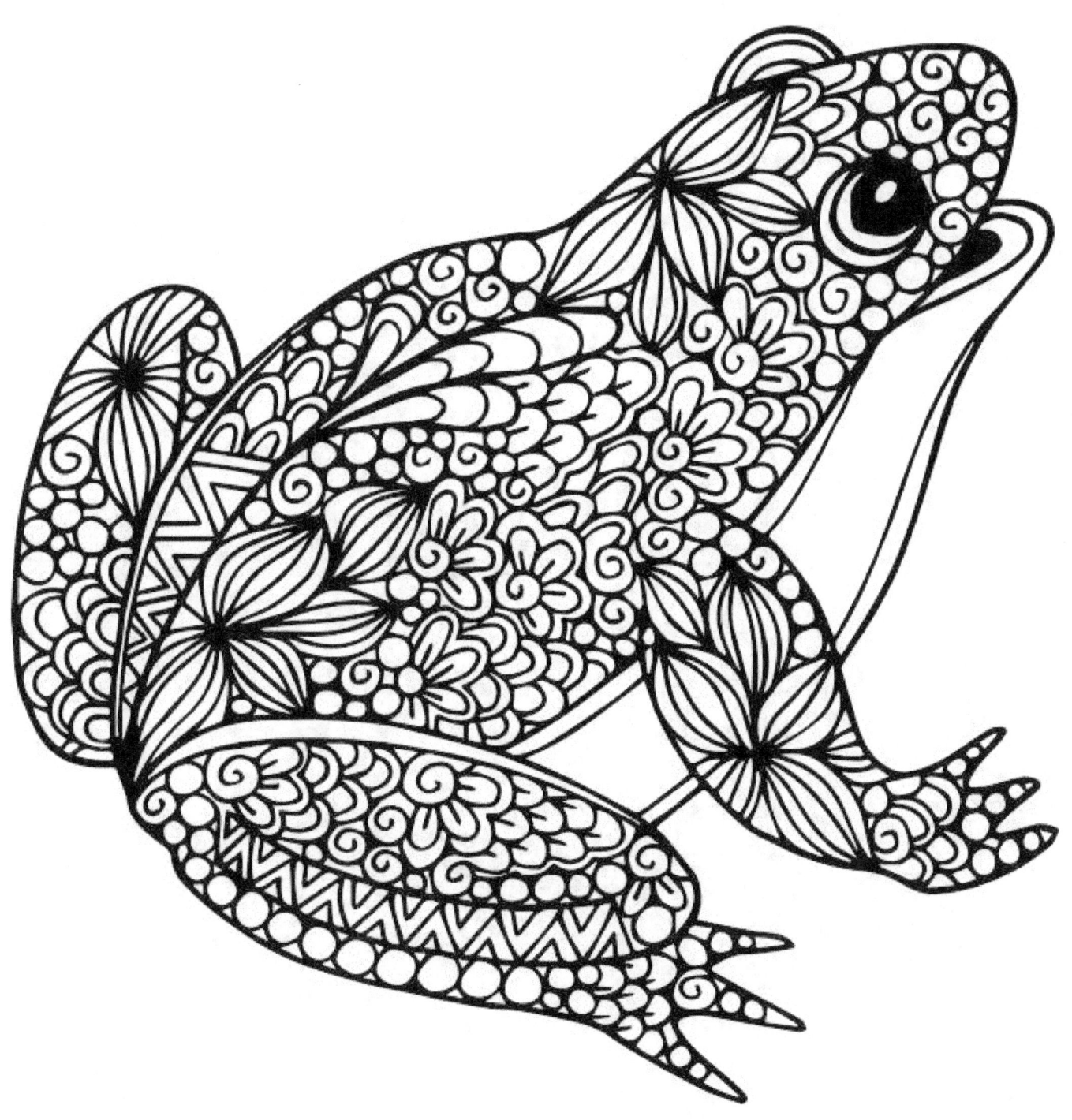

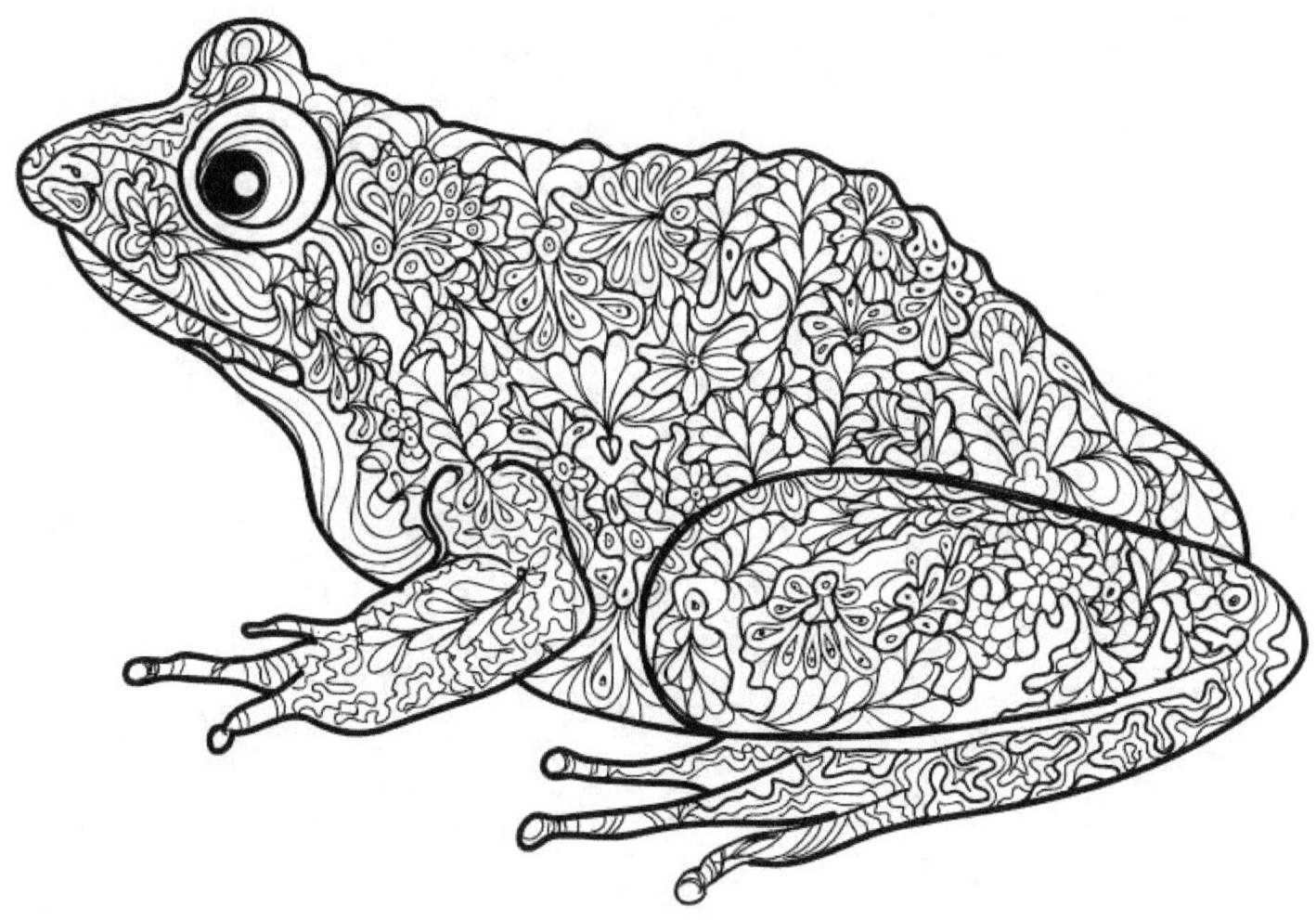

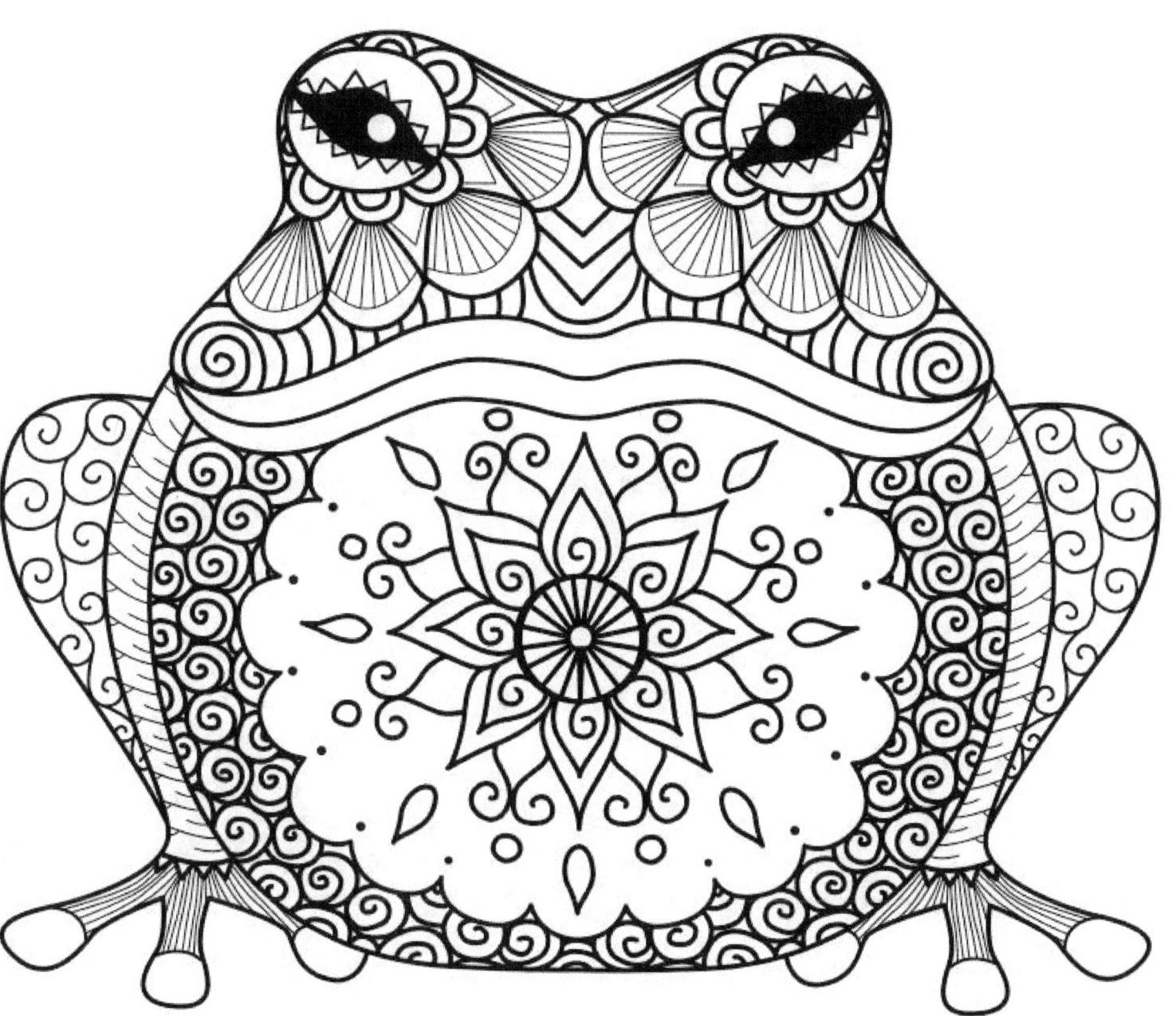

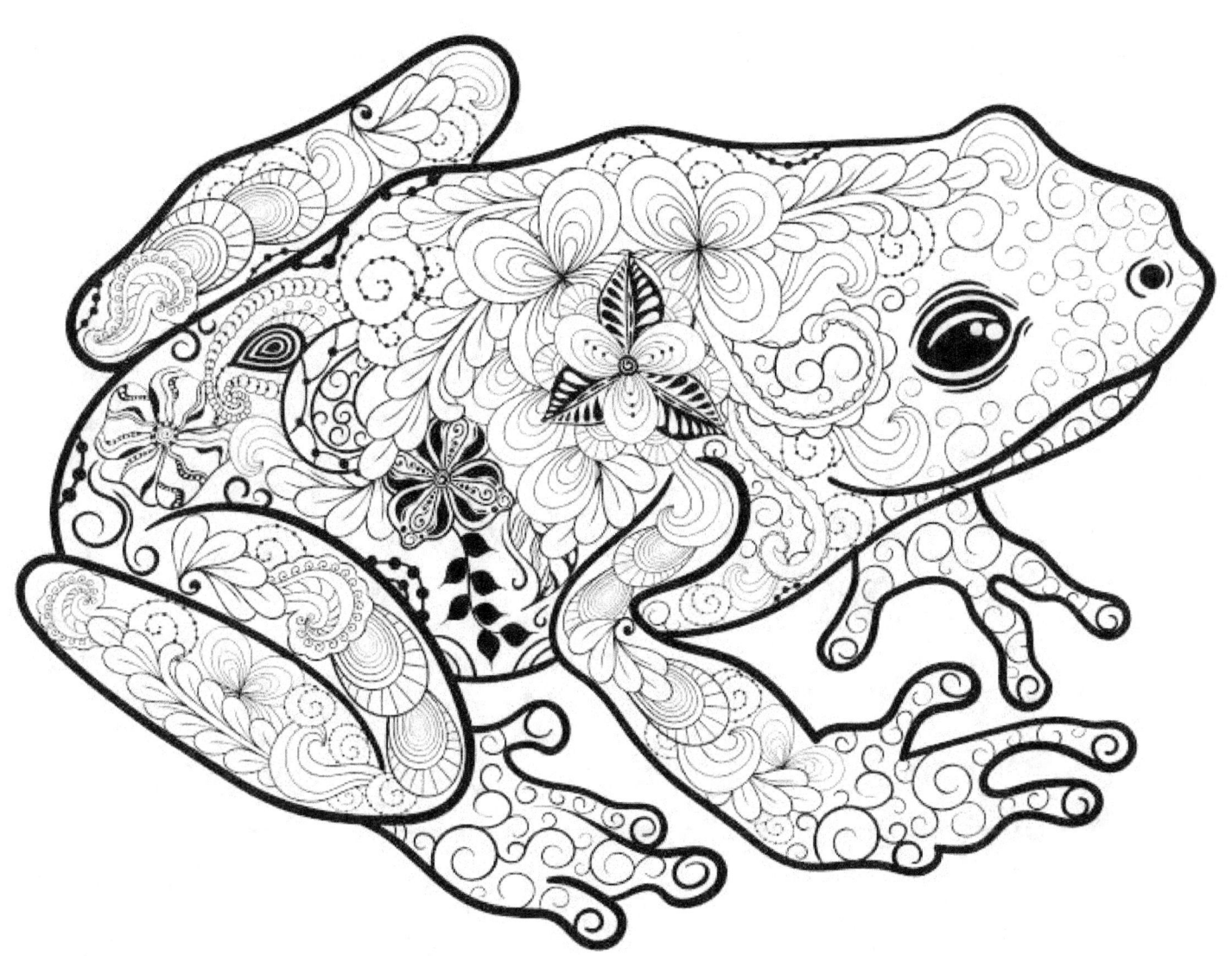

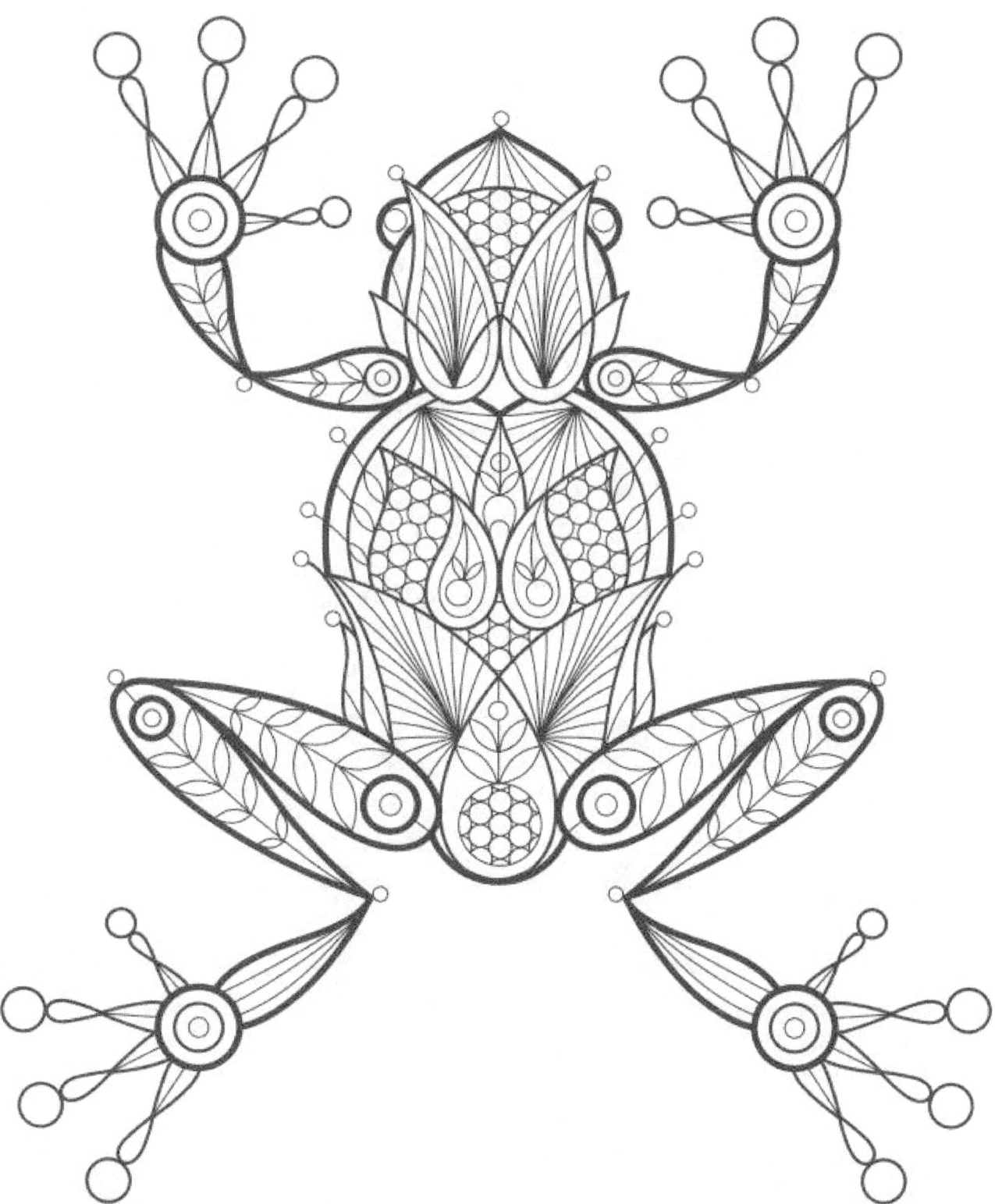

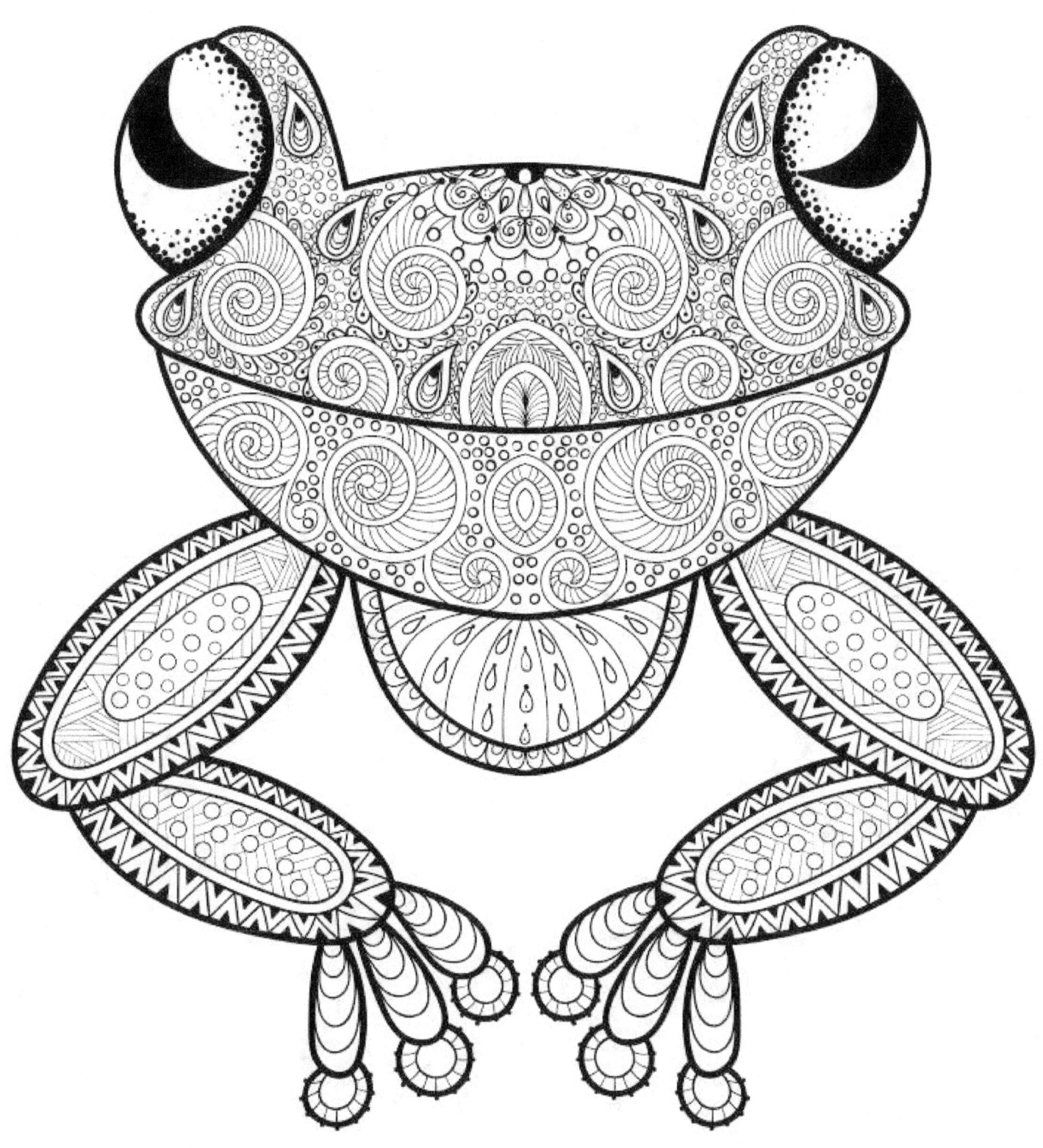

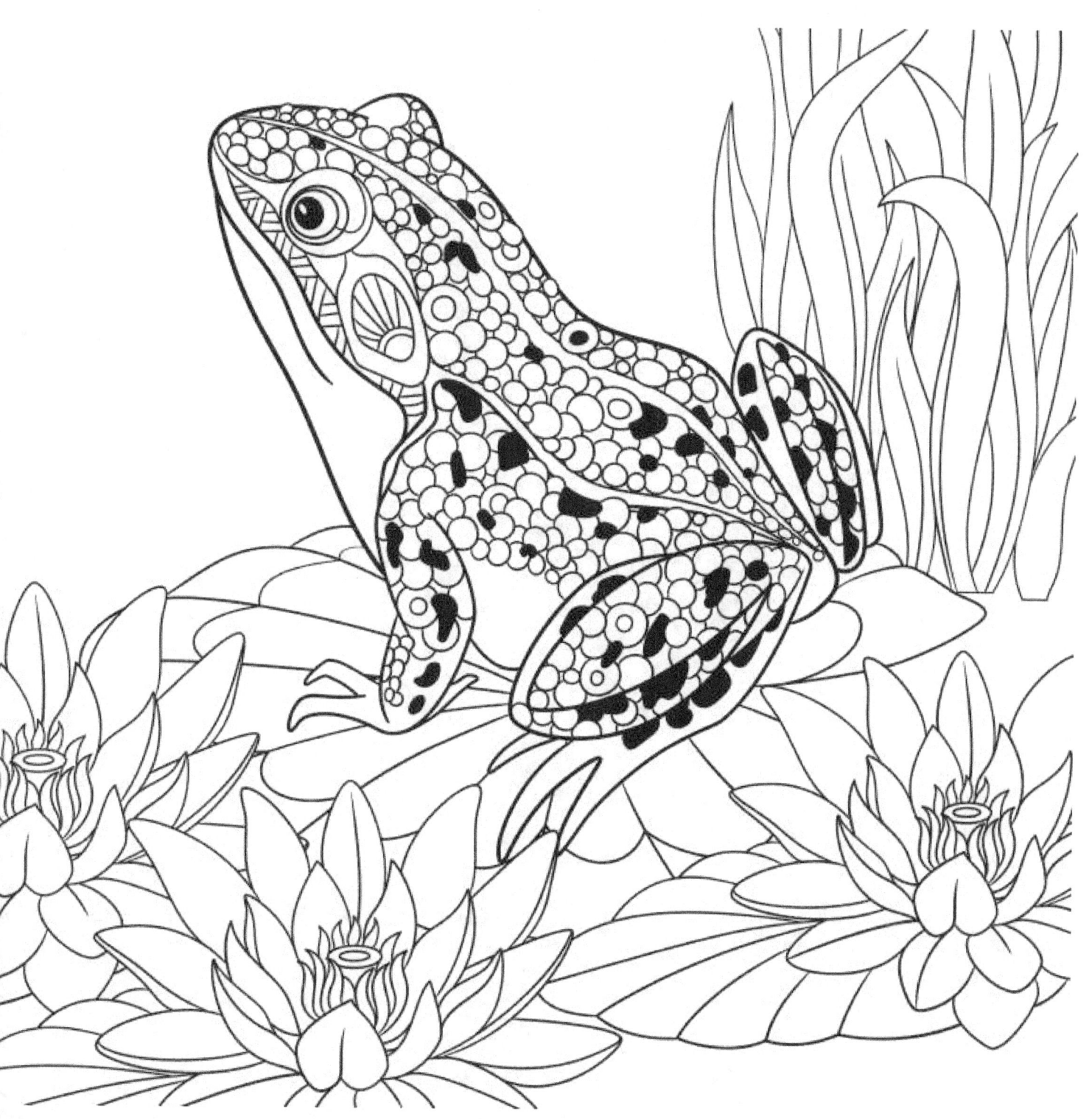

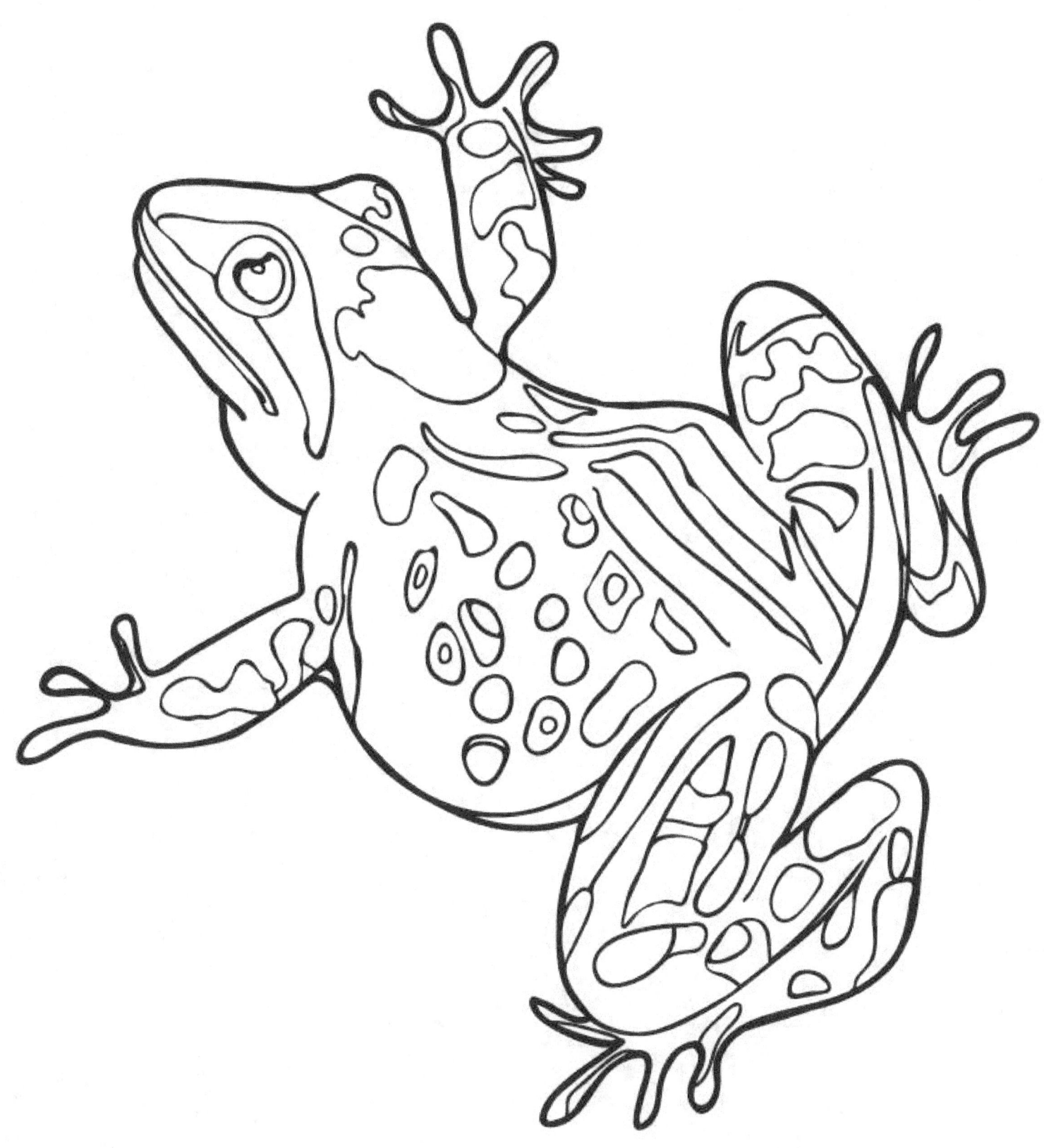

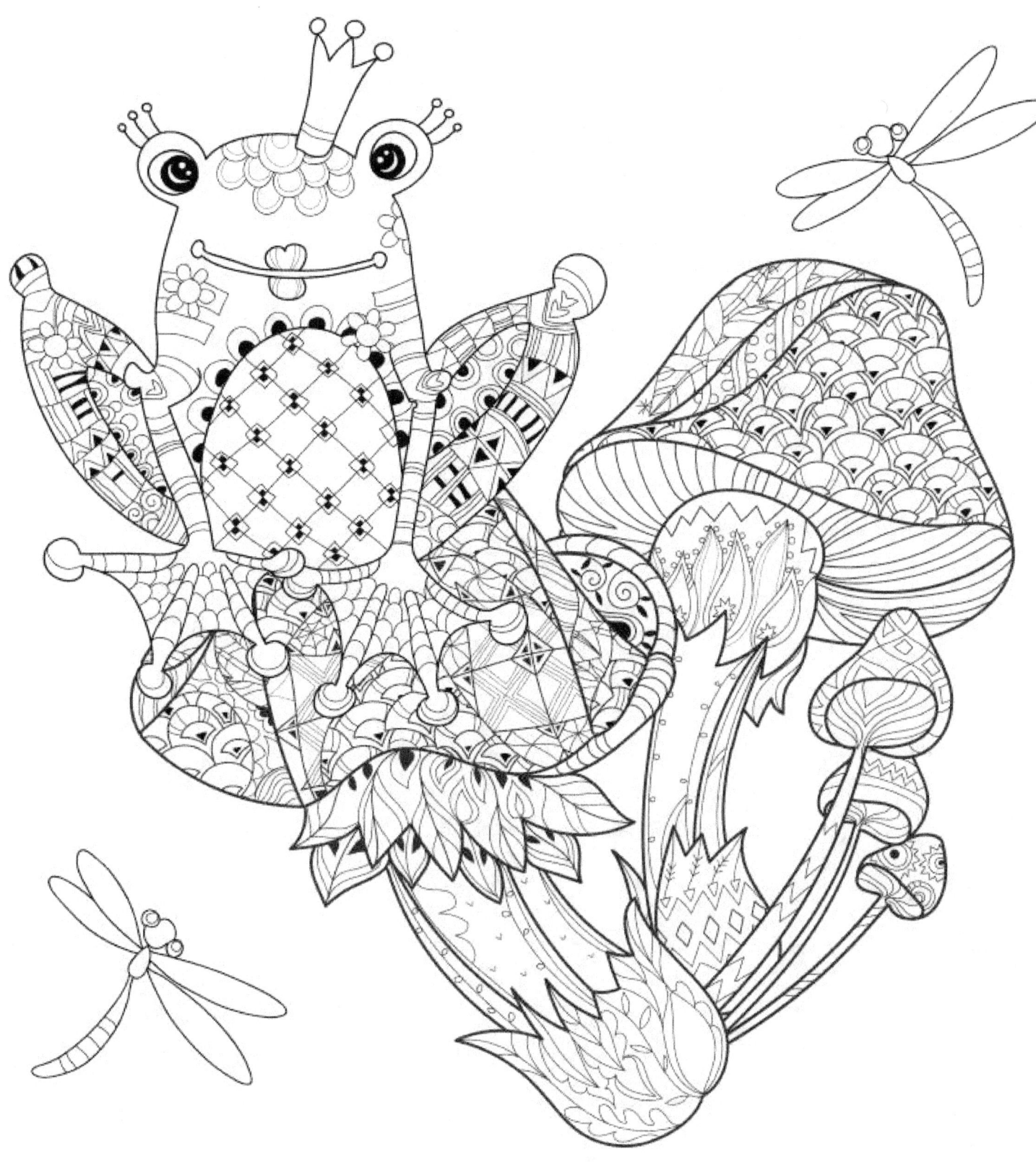

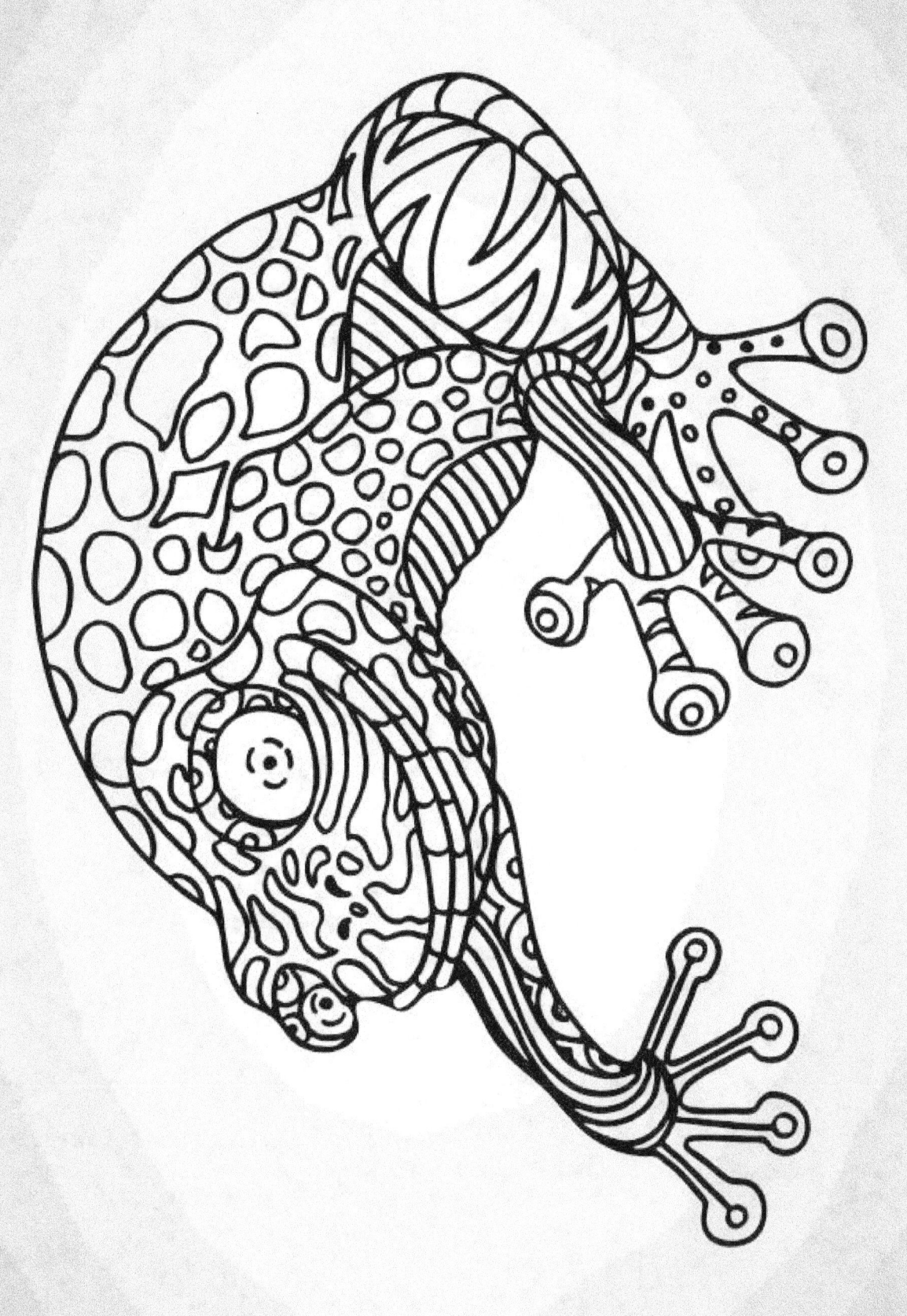

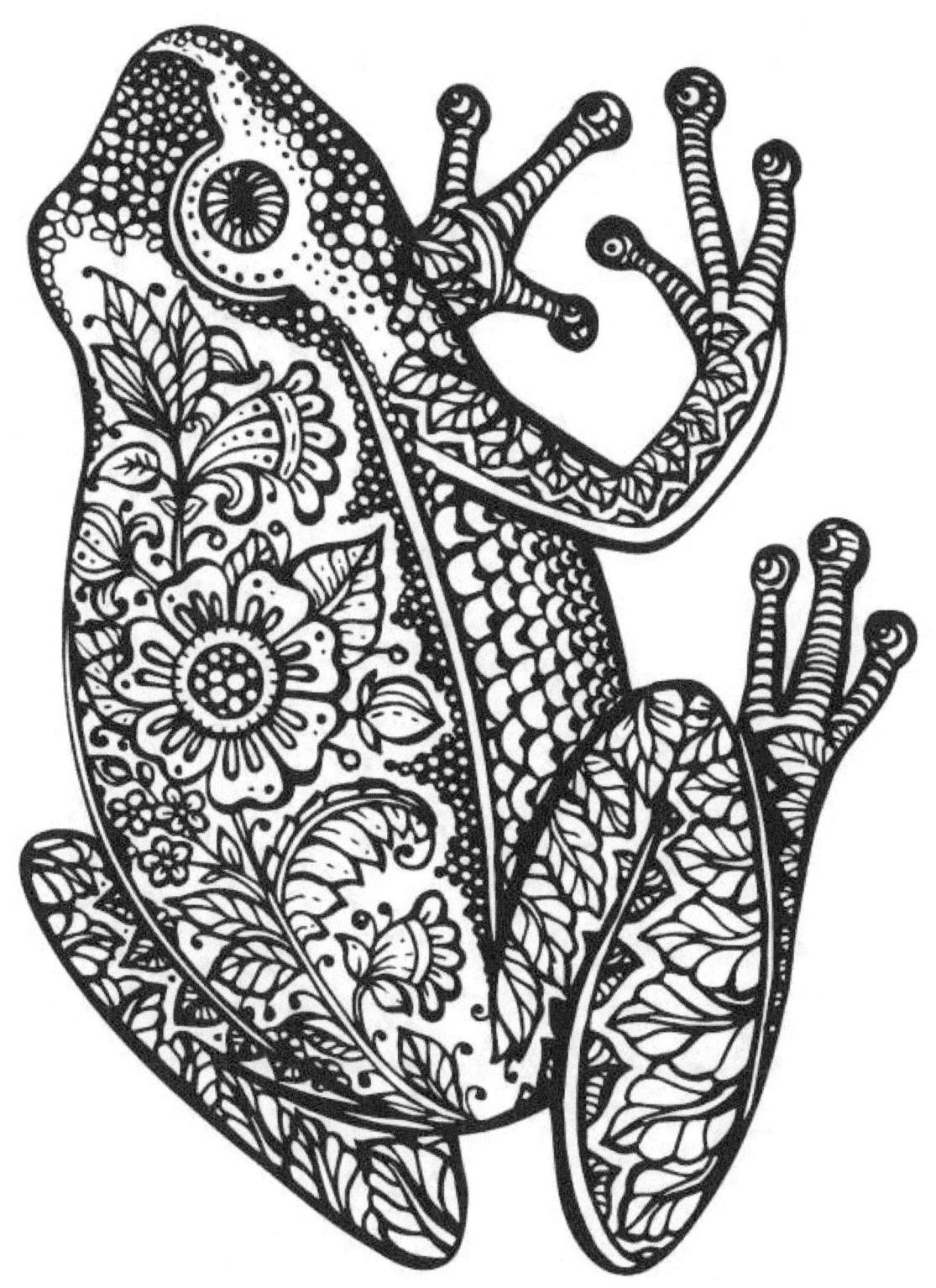

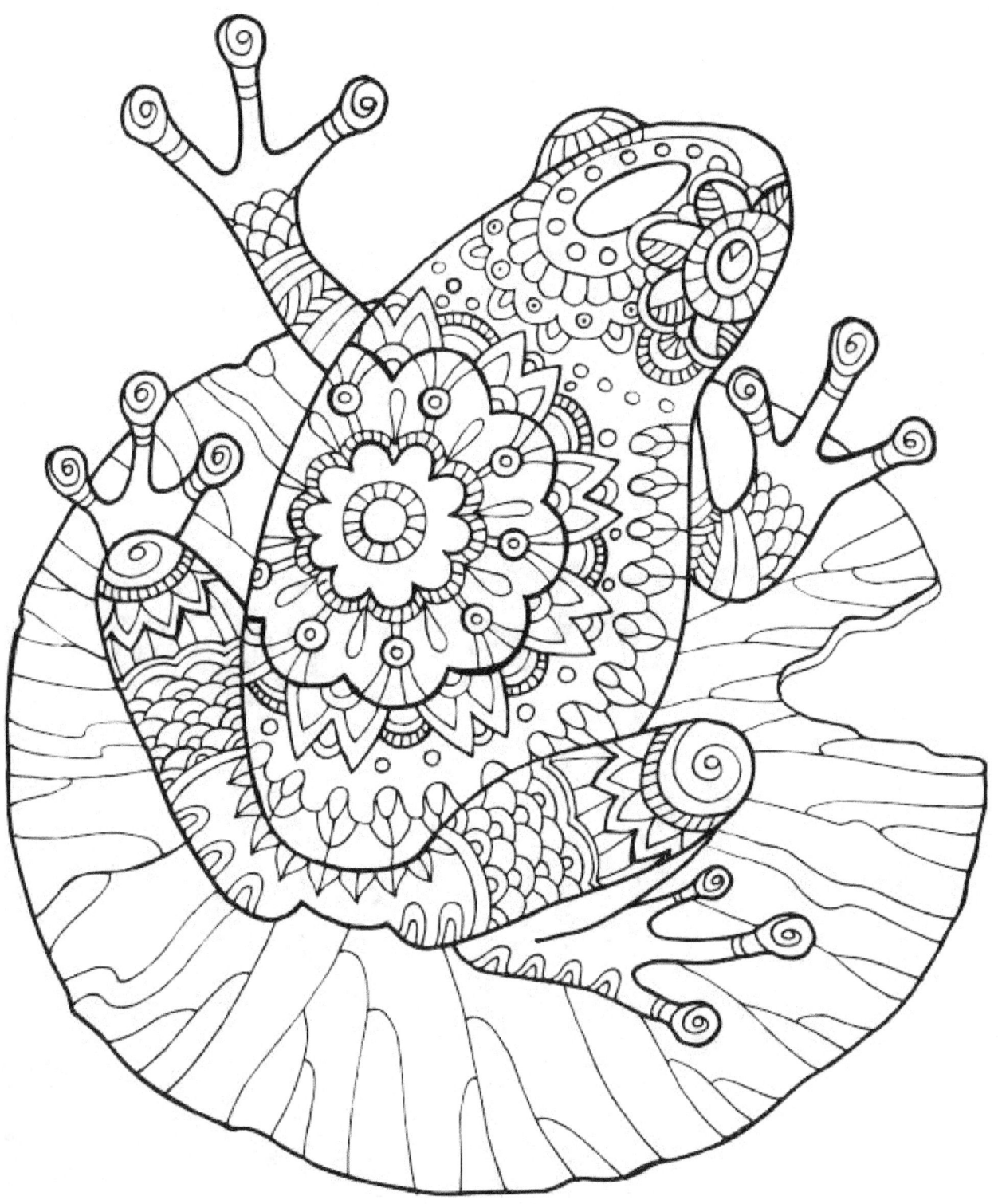

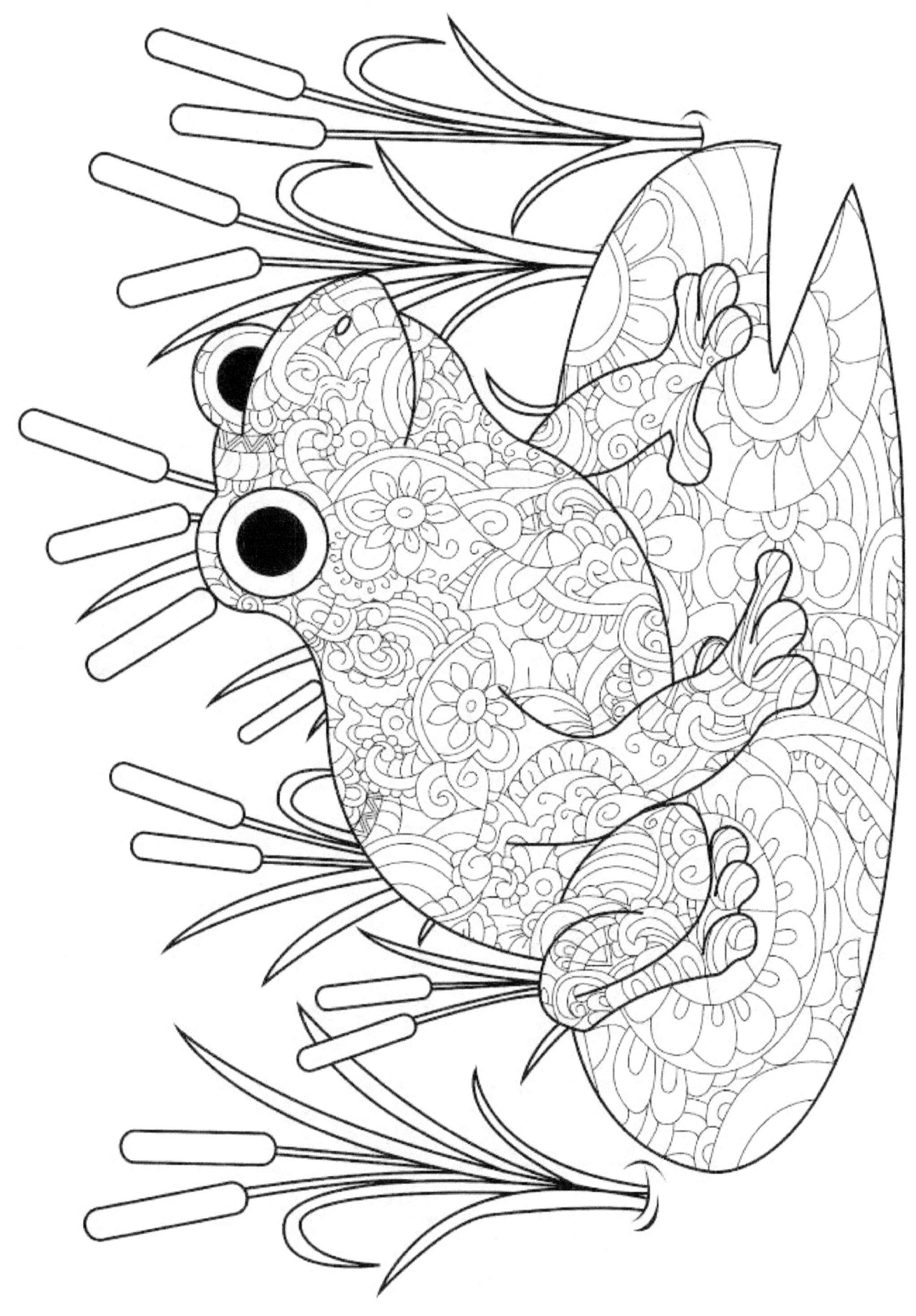

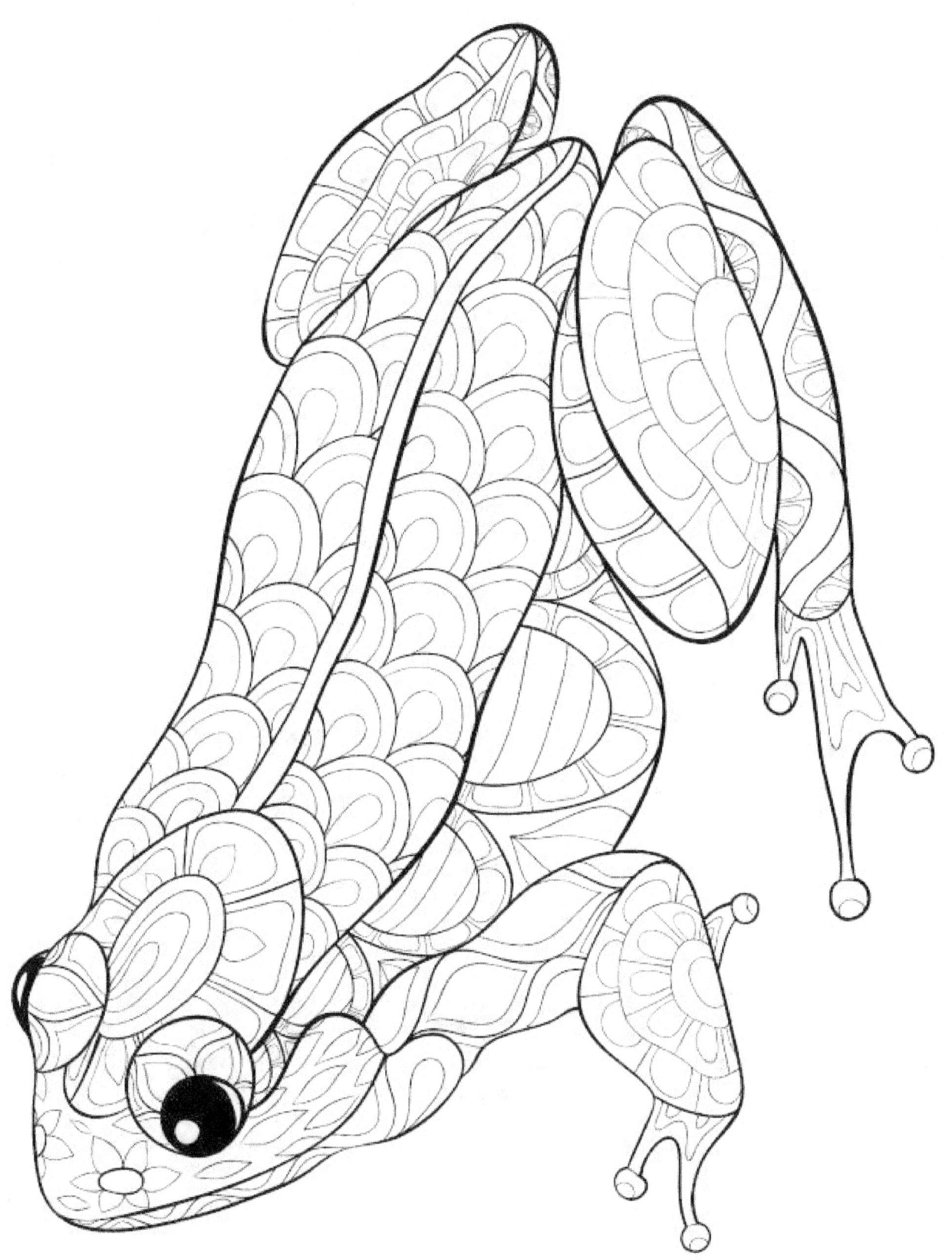

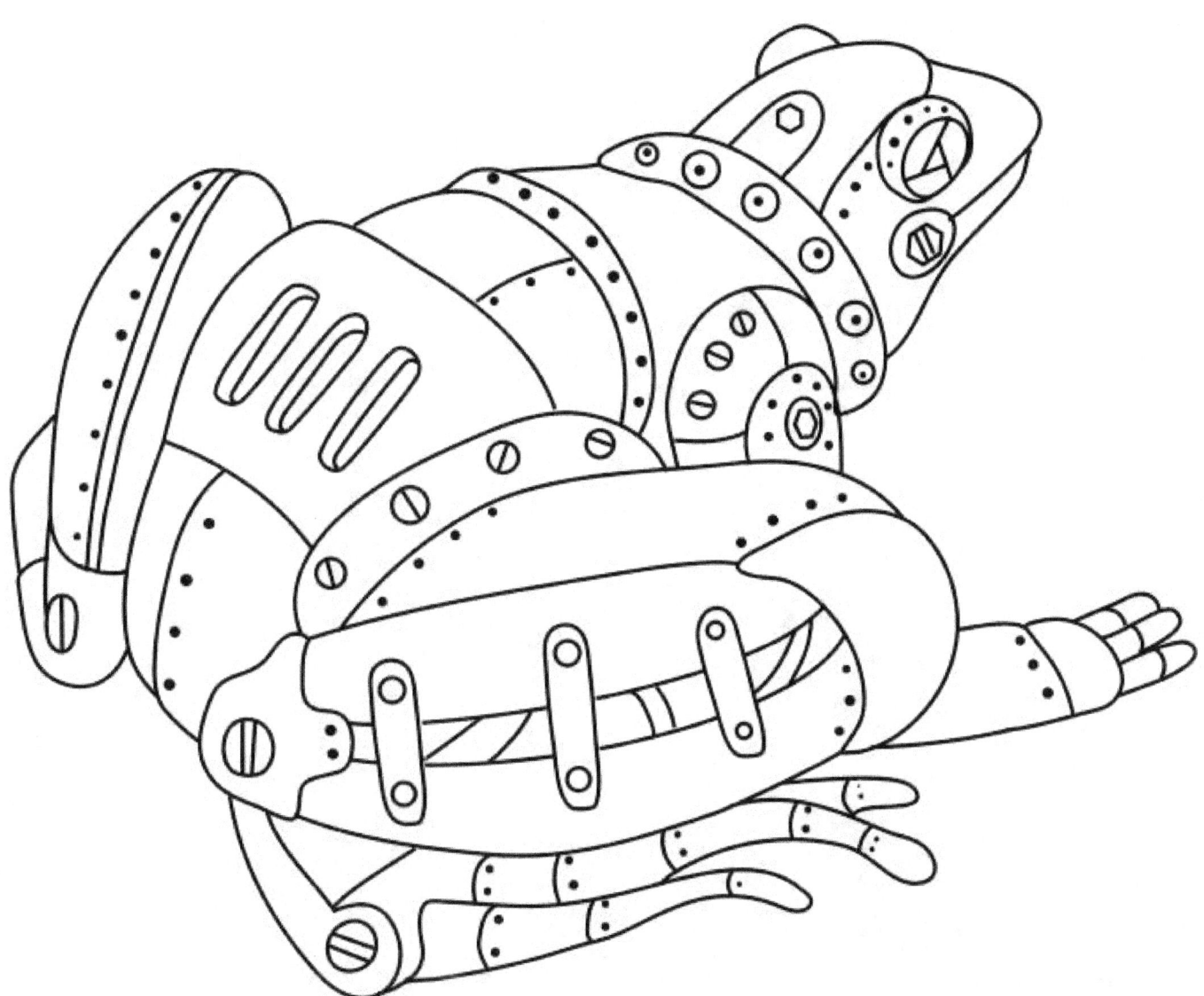

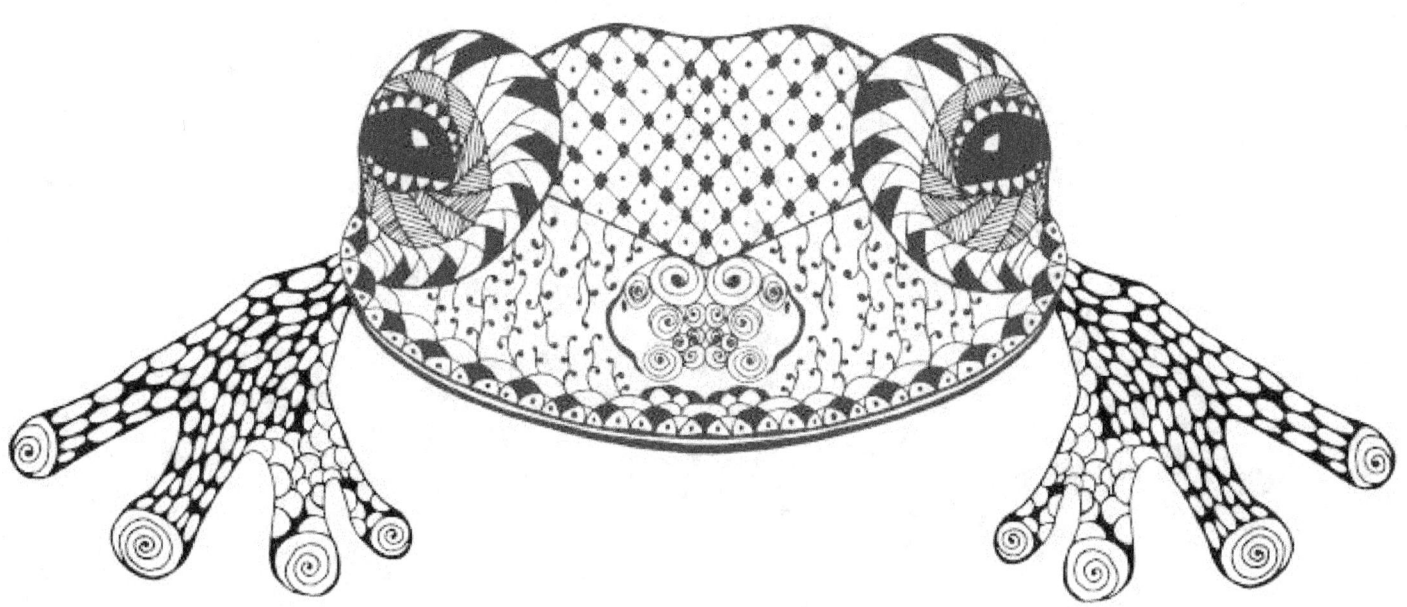

Surprise Bonus Sea Turtles Coloring Pages!

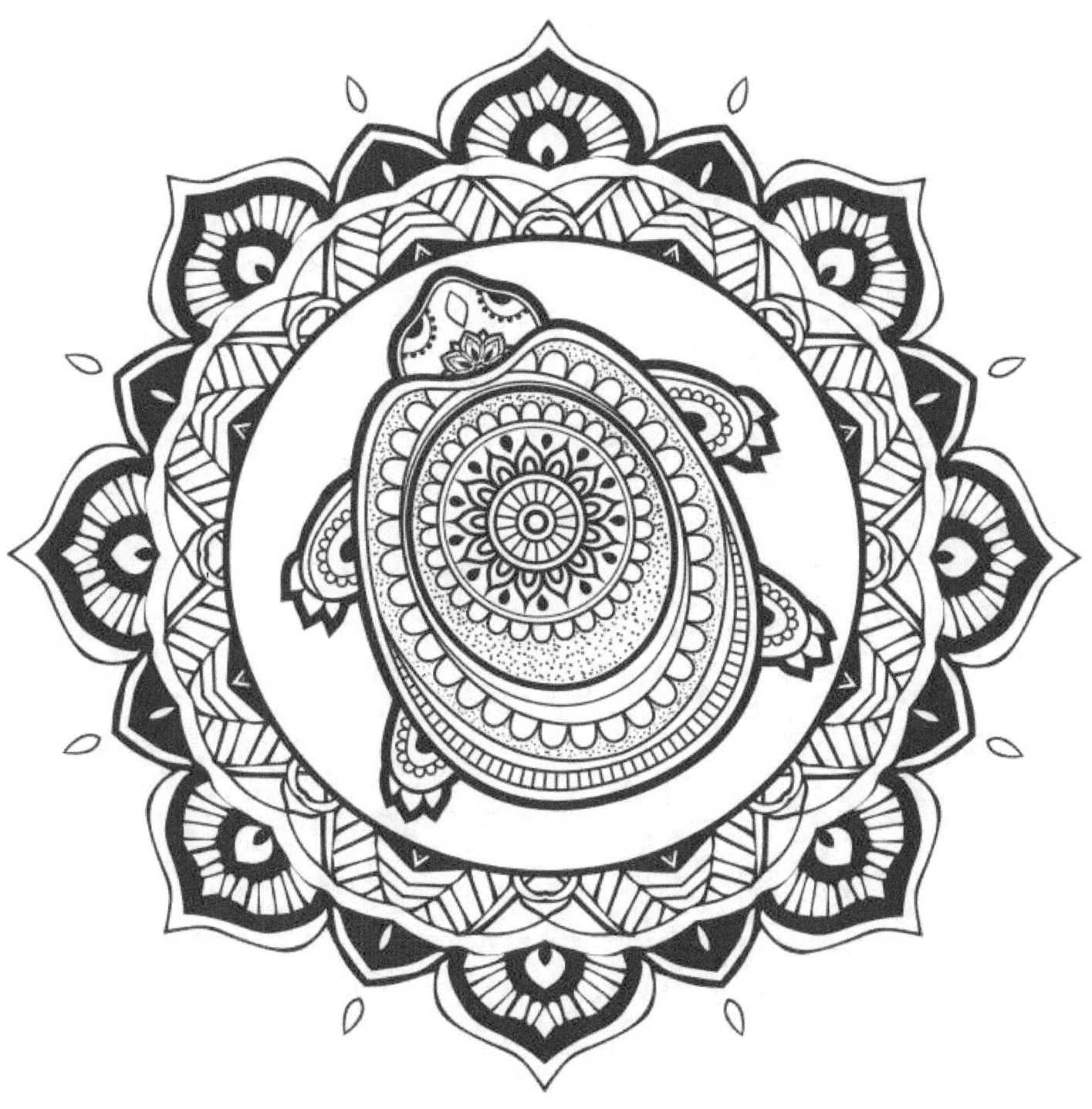

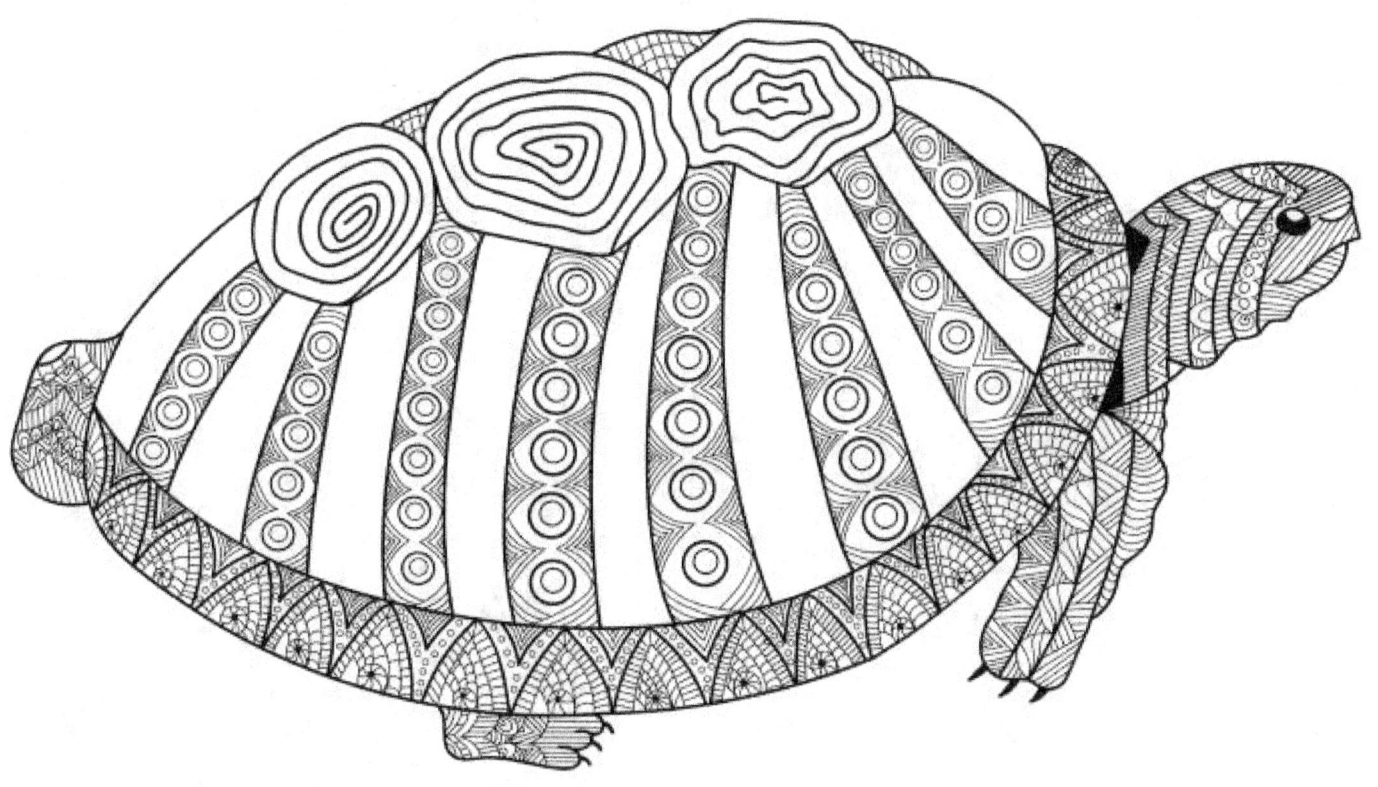

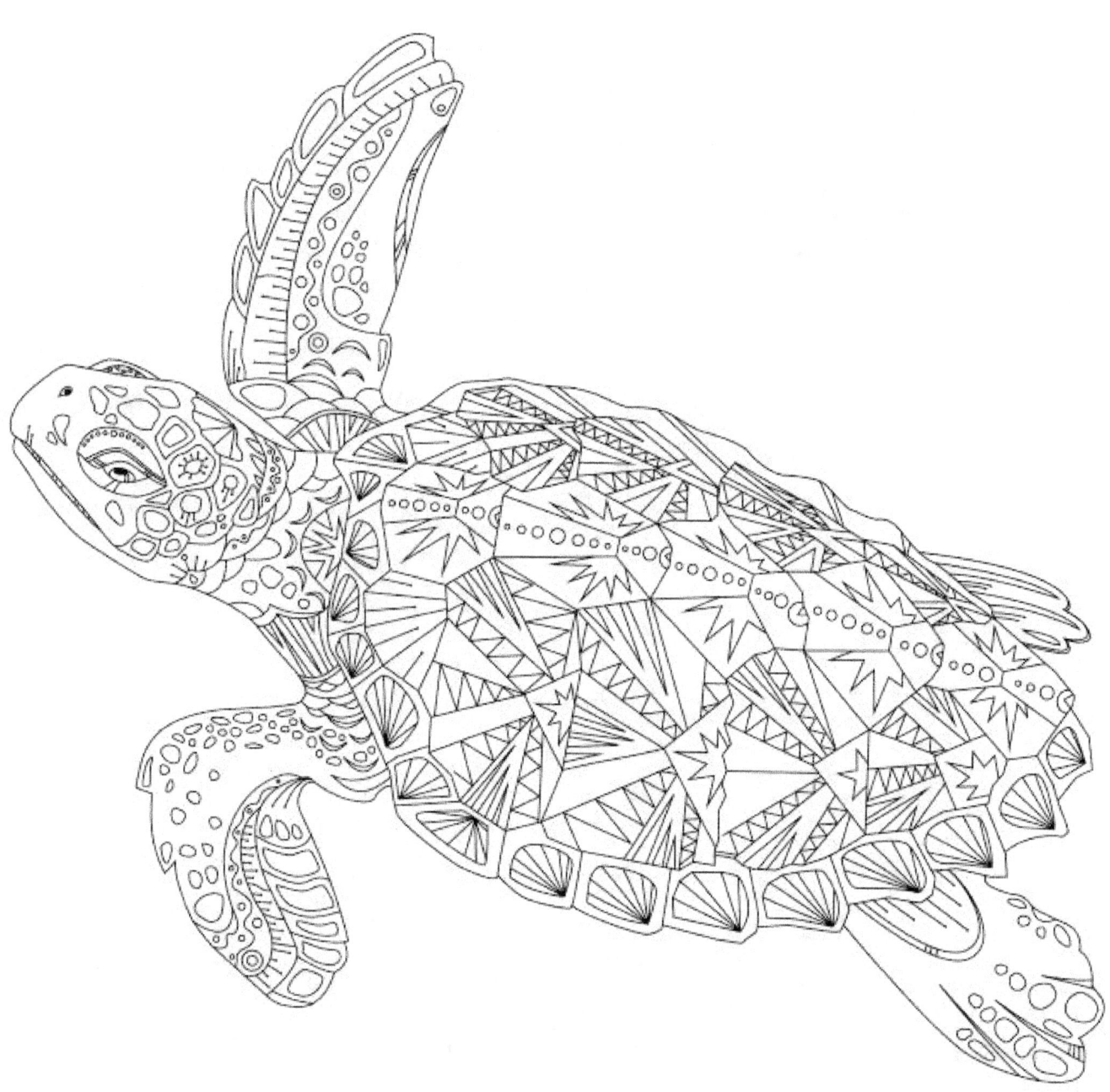

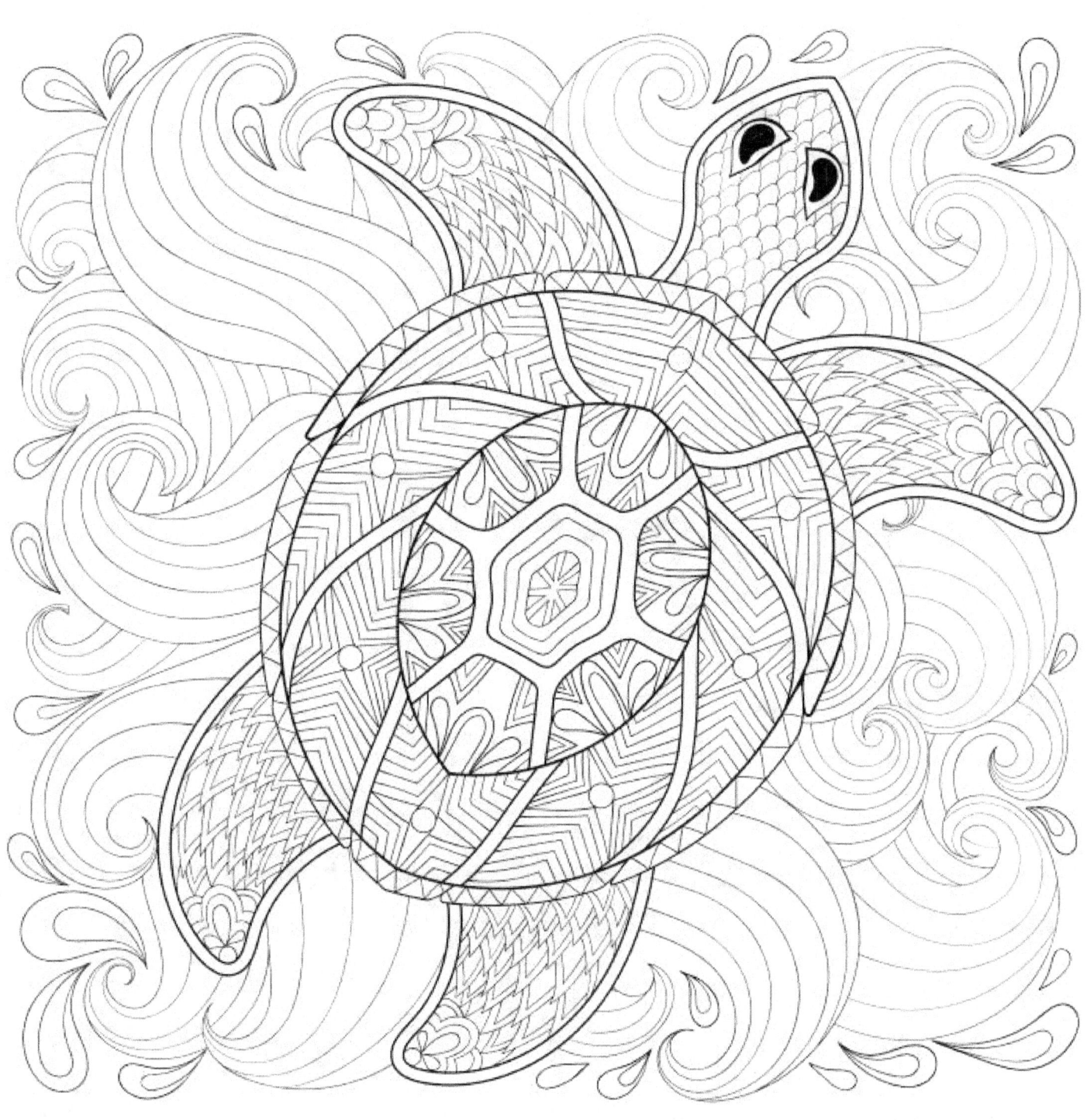

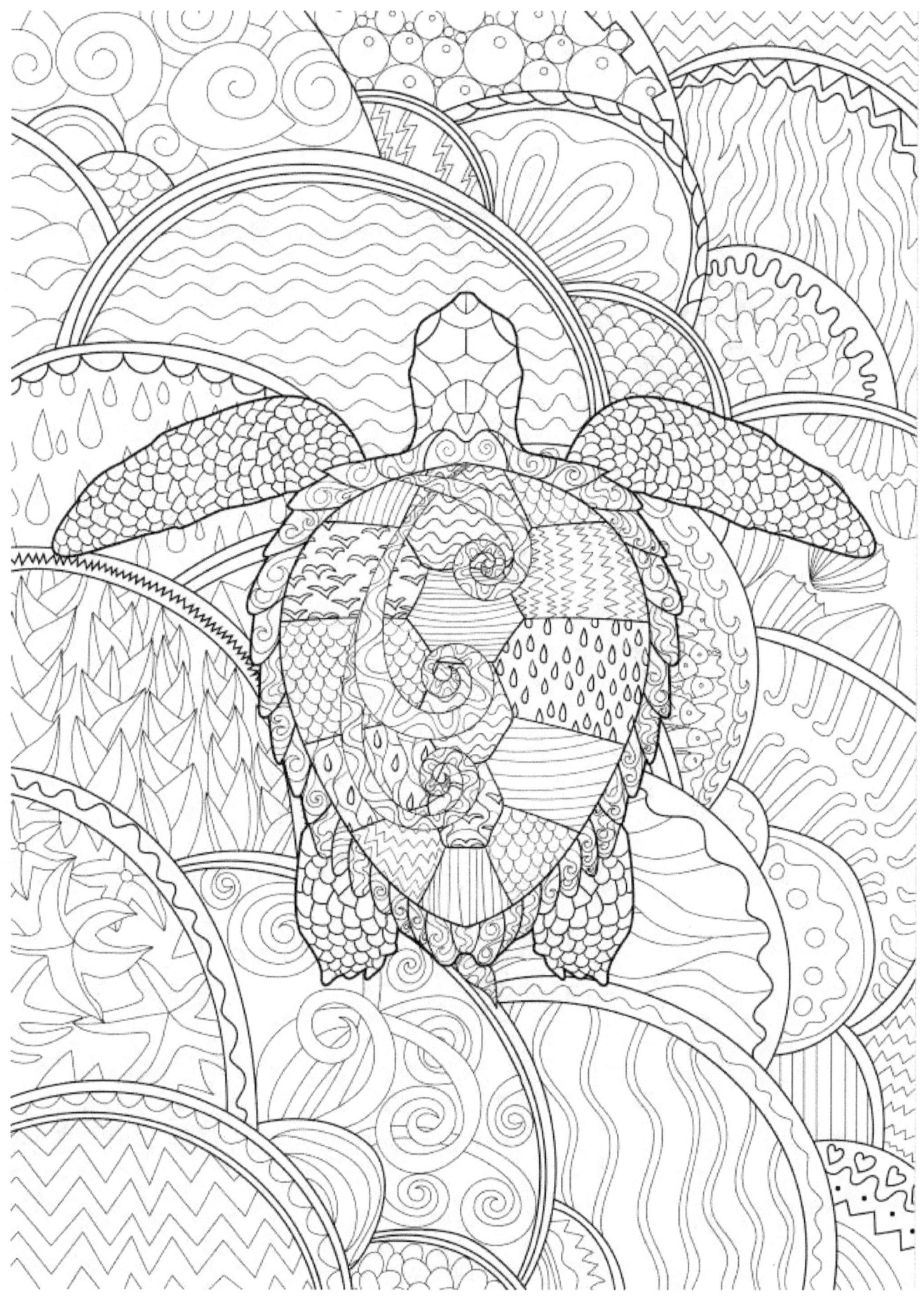

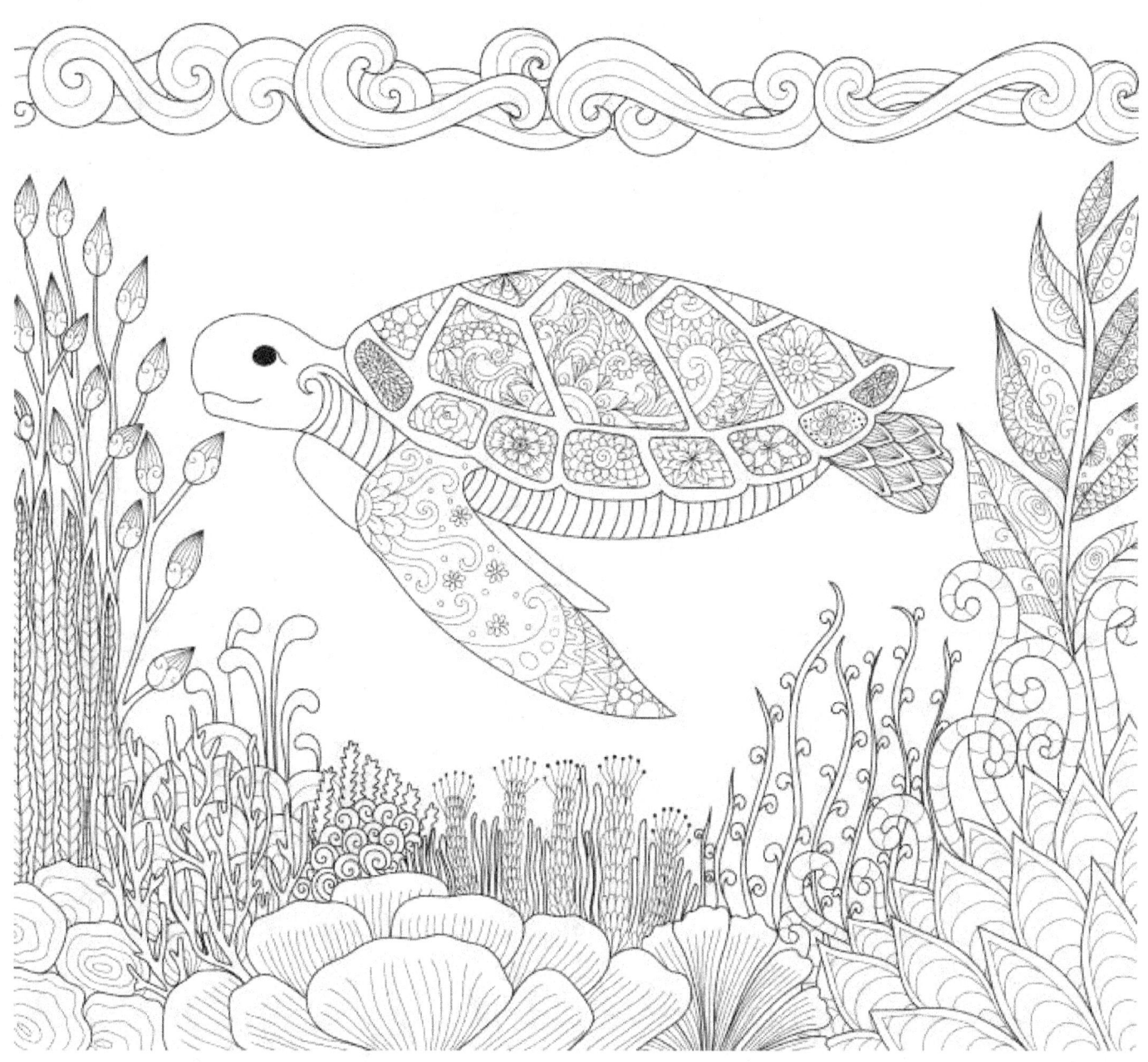

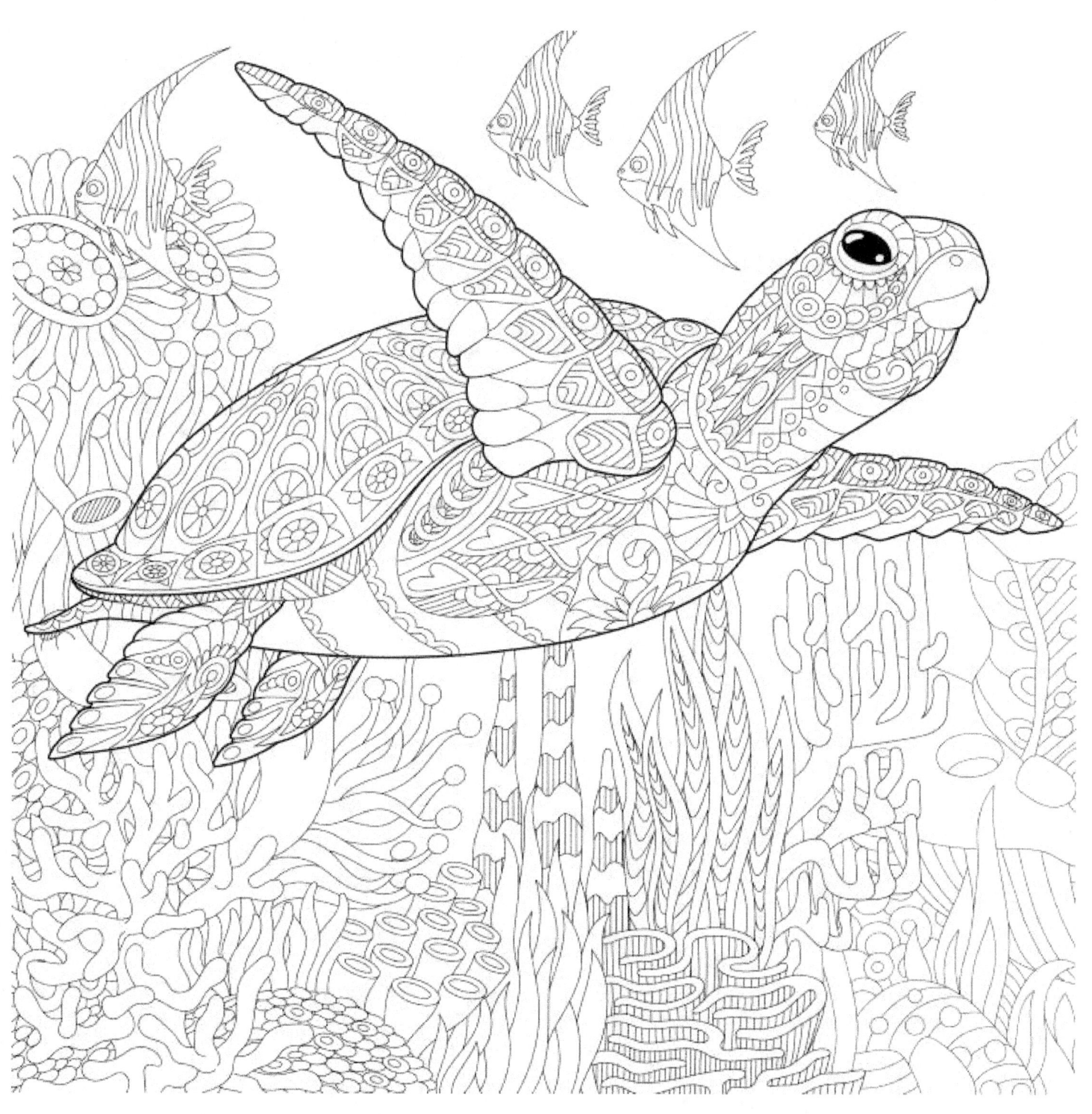

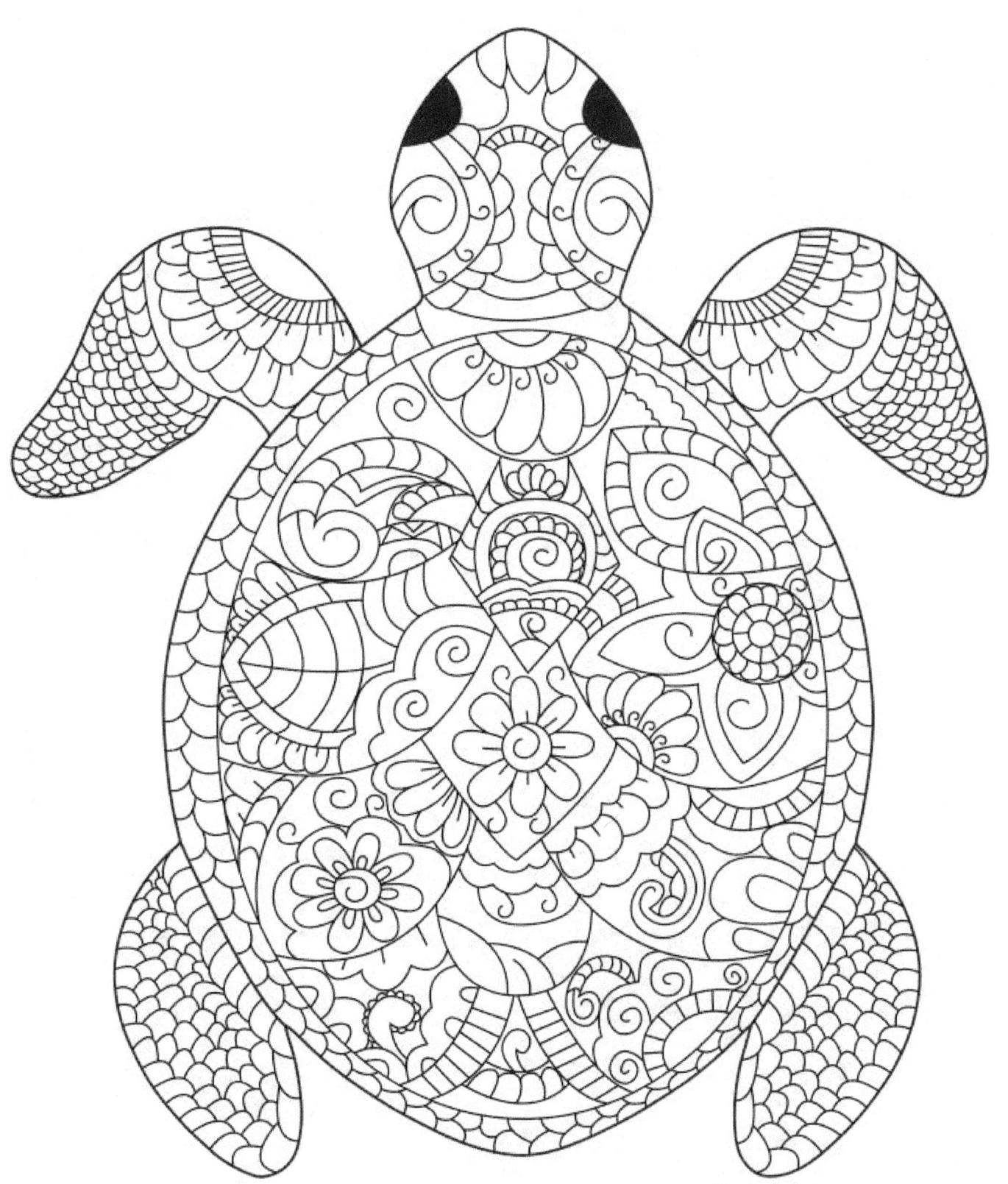

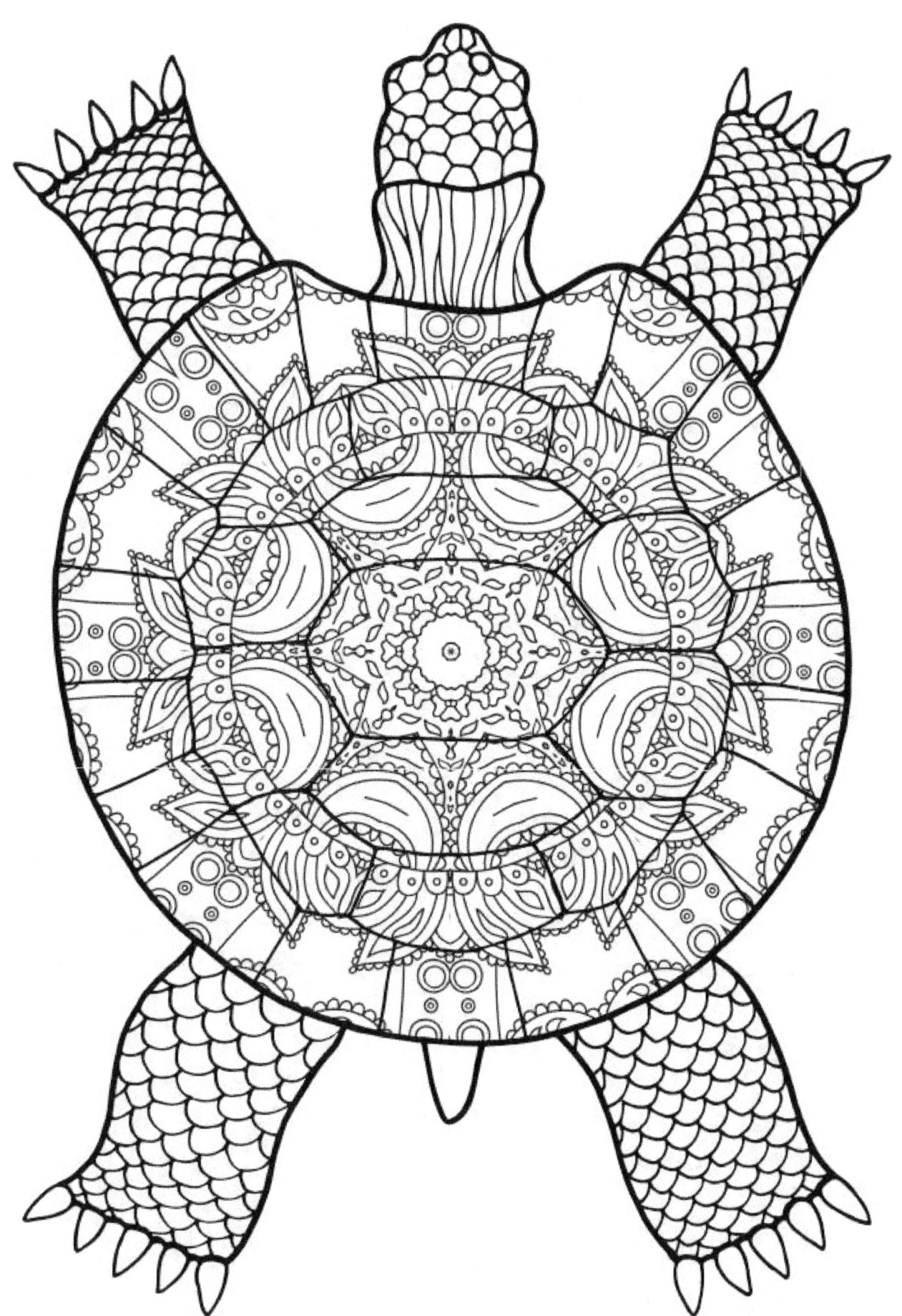

www.ingramcontent.com/pod-product-compliance
Lightning Source LLC
Chambersburg PA
CBHW081211180526
45170CB00006B/2296